100
Amazing
Answers
to Prayer

William J. Petersen served as editorial director of *Christian Life* magazine and *Christian Bookseller* magazine before becoming editor of *Eternity* magazine. A past president of the Evangelical Press Association, he was the first recipient of the Joseph T. Bayly Award, for "outstanding service to Christian periodical publishing." He was awarded a doctorate by Eastern College for his contributions to religious journalism.

He was editorial director of the *Revell Bible Dictionary* and has written Bible study curricula and Bible study aids for various curricula and Bible publishers. He has written more than twenty books on various subjects, including biography, Bible study, cults, hymnology, and travel. With his son Randy Petersen he has written four previous books: *The One Year Book of Hymns*, *The One Year Book of Psalms*, *100 Christian Books That Changed the Century*, and *100 Bible Verses That Changed the World*.

Bill and his wife, Ardythe, are the parents of three grown children and live in Pennsylvania, where he continues to serve as senior acquisitions editor of Fleming H. Revell.

Randy Petersen has served as editor of the *Bible Newsletter* and on the staff of *Christian History Magazine*. He was content editor of the *Revell Bible Dictionary* and has written a considerable amount of Bible study curricula for youth and adults. He is the author of more than thirty books and was coauthor of *The 100 Most Important Events in Church History*, *100 Christian Books That Changed the Century*, and *100 Bible Verses That Changed the World*. His other books range from *How to Fear God without Being Afraid of Him* and *Angry with God* to *The Family Book of Bible Fun* and *The Complete Book of Bible Puzzles*. He has also written books dealing with sports and psychology, devotionals, and fiction. Active in his Methodist church in New Jersey, Randy also acts, directs, and teaches in local theaters and schools.

100
Amazing
Answers
to Prayer

William J. Petersen
and Randy Petersen

Fleming H. Revell
A Division of Baker Book House Co
Grand Rapids, Michigan 49516

Published by Fleming H. Revell
a division of Baker Book House Company
P.O. Box 6287, Grand Rapids, MI 49516-6287
www.bakerbooks.com

Printed in the United States of America

Library of Congress Cataloging-in-Publication Data
Petersen, William J.
    100 amazing answers to prayer / William J. Petersen and Randy Petersen.
        p.   cm.
    Includes bibliographical references.
        ISBN 0-8007-5831-5
    1. Prayer—Christianity. I. Petersen, Randy. II. Title.
    BV220 .P48 2003
    248.3′2—dc21   2002012776

If you know of an amazing answer to prayer, we would be interested in hearing about it. Please e-mail your story to amazingprayers@aol.com. We would like to consider it for inclusion in a future edition of *100 Amazing Answers to Prayer*. By submitting your answer to prayer, you acknowledge that you are giving us permission to edit and use it if we select it for future publication. Of course, we cannot guarantee that we will be able to use your answer to prayer, but you can be sure that we will read and carefully consider it.

Contents

1

Our Amazing God

Where did we get the idea that we could ask the almighty God to do things and he would? From the Bible, that's where. Elijah's prayers bring fire from the sky. Hezekiah's actually add ten years to his life. "Ask and you shall receive," Jesus promises. "Let your requests be made known to God," says Paul. "The effective, fervent prayer of a righteous person accomplishes a great deal," adds James.

So prayer works—at least it's supposed to. The hundred examples in this book would seem to verify that fact. Given enough time and resources, you could hunt down a hundred *thousand* examples. Things happen when Christians pray. Strange things. Things that make you laugh. Things that make you go *hmmmm.*

We begin to step into dangerous territory, however, when we say that prayer "works." If we treat prayer like a genie in a magic lamp, we miss the point. Prayer is not about getting what we wish for. It's a whole process of connecting with a personal God who cares about our wants and needs but also has his own exciting plans for us.

That's what you'll see in these one hundred examples. These prayers weren't prayed by people who just used God to get what they craved. Those praying were practicing an ongoing relationship with God. As in any relationship, they cared about what God wanted, and God cared about what they wanted and needed.

You can't put God in a box; he won't fit. And if you try to turn him into a machine that operates at the push of a button, you'll be disappointed. All sorts of people have tried to figure out the formula for effective prayer. Do you have to kneel, bow your head, close your eyes, fold your hands, or say, "In Jesus' name, amen"? Nothing's wrong with any of those actions, of course, but we can't expect them to force God's hand. Jesus talked about the "pagans" who prayed in empty babblings, thinking they would be heard just because they talked a lot. We often take the same superstitious approach.

Powerful prayer is always rooted in *relationship*. Oh, we might get a few of our push-button prayers answered, but we'll probably get far more than we bargained for, because God is far more than a divine butler. He answers prayers when he wants and how he chooses, and he reveals himself to us as he answers.

Jesus often referred to the importance of faith in our prayers. "Believe that you have received it," he reminded us. Even a mustard seed of faith would move mountains. Does that mean some prayers go unanswered because some of us can't drum up even a mustard seed of faith? Some might say so, but we disagree.

Such an approach simply puts the focus back on us, as if we earn answers to our prayers by believing hard enough. Indeed, many Christians attempt all sorts of mental and spiritual gymnastics to convince themselves that they have unwavering, absolutely confident, no-shred-of-doubt faith. But God always operates within an economy of grace. Jesus worked a miracle for the man who said, "I believe. Help my unbelief."

Faith is like a light switch. Does a light switch make the lights go on? Yes and no. Yes, it has that effect, but no, it doesn't create the power for the lights. The electrical current does that. By flipping the switch, you allow the current to get to the light and empower it. In the same way, faith allows the power of God to work in a situation. The prayer of faith is effective not because of the spiritual power of the person praying, but because of the power of God. Faith simply throws the switch. As Paul put it, "We are saved by grace through faith." Grace provides the power; faith lets it through.

Remember, biblical faith is personal. Faith is more than just believing *that;* it's believing *in.* I can believe *that* a certain chair is sturdy, but I don't believe *in* it until I sit on it. Similarly, I can believe *that* God will answer a prayer, but do I truly believe *in* the goodness of the answering God?

This kind of faith is not manipulation. God is not a machine into which you pour magic words of faith and out comes your answer! No, in prayer we commit our desires to God: "Here's what is in my heart, Lord."

This brings us back to relationship. Our petitions take their place alongside praise, thanks, and confession as a natural part of our interaction with God. As we would with any close friend, we express our concerns about the events of our lives, but recognizing the power of our great God, we ask him to work mightily within our lives. We can ask for an outcome we desire, but we also understand that he might have a better idea. We count on God's wisdom to edit our requests and to give us what's truly good for us. Paul said it long ago: We don't know what to pray for. Thank God that his Spirit translates our requests into better ones.

So prayerful faith is not necessarily the belief that God will do exactly what we ask but the trust that he will hear our desires and do what's best for us.

As you read these accounts of Christians whose prayers were answered, should you hail these people as giants of faith? Not exactly. Sure, some famous Christians are included here, and a slew of missionaries, but lots of ordinary folks appear as well. No doubt these are fine, faithful people, but keep the focus on the grace of the answering God rather than on the merits of the askers.

God has always delighted in showing grace to the most unlikely recipients—the needy, the poor in spirit. You don't need

11

to be a spiritual star to see God work in and around your life. You just need to ask. After all is said and done, we still don't understand why the eternal God deigns to answer our prayers, but he does. Again and again, he hears from heaven and grants our meager petitions.

That is truly amazing.

2

Prayer in the Hot Spots

How God Works in and around the Headlines

If my people, who are called by my name, will humble themselves and pray and seek my face and turn from their wicked
ways, then will I hear from heaven and will forgive their sin and
will heal their land.

2 Chronicles 7:14

Does prayer have an impact on world events?

God's abilities are never in question. Almighty God can work
wonders great and small.

We're cautious in our answer, however, because there are
many miracles he chooses not to perform. Despite numerous
prayers for world peace, wars keep popping up. As frustrating
as it is for us, God allows people to wage war, kidnap people,
and do all kinds of wicked things. Why? We're not going to
tackle that issue in these pages.

Yet we do know that God works in and around those events,
sometimes protecting his people, often providing comfort, reg-

13

ularly touching individual lives within the crises. When a group of people unites in prayer and allows God's truth to filter through them, God has been known to extend his mighty arm and tilt the course of history. In recent decades we have seen the fall of an atheistic Communist regime in Europe and of an oppressive apartheid policy in South Africa. Both events were unthinkable just a few years before they happened. Both were matters of prayer.

"Thy kingdom come . . . ," we pray, "on earth as it is in heaven." And sometimes God becomes a major player in world politics. But Jesus also reminded us, "My kingdom is not of this world" (John 18:36a). Often he chooses to weave his kingdom out of the threads of individual hearts and prayers.

> *O Lord,*
> *never suffer us to think*
> *that we can stand by ourselves,*
> *and not need Thee.*
>
> John Donne

Kabul

Unlocking the Taliban Prison

Two young American women arrested in Afghanistan by the Taliban, the headlines blared on August 3, 2001. *Relief workers charged with spreading Christianity.* When the Antioch Community Church of Waco, Texas, heard that Dayna Curry and Heather Mercer had been detained, they began praying nonstop for their release.

Dayna and Heather had been members of the Antioch church since they were students at Baylor University. When

14

the two women joined Shelter Now, a non-profit aid organization in Kabul, Afghanistan, the church supported their ministry with money and prayer. Pastor Jimmy Seibert said the two woman had "an incredible heart for the people of Afghanistan. They have gone there to love Afghans by serving in practical ways, from feeding programs to education to health care. We are proud of the work that they do, and we are proud to be a part of their lives."

> Prayer gives you courage to make the decisions you must make in a crisis and then the confidence to leave the result to a Higher Power.
>
> Dwight Eisenhower

The details leading to the arrest are still somewhat murky. Curry admitted she gave a book about Jesus to an Afghan boy and showed his family a film about Christ because they expressed interest. Yet such proselytizing is illegal in that land. "If they have broken the law and should be hanged," the Taliban's chief justice said, "then we will punish them like that."

For a month after their arrest, the two young women were cut off from the outside world. Their attorney was in Pakistan, and they were unable to reach him for weeks. At their first prison, six women were confined to a ten-foot-by-ten-foot cell, and when six mattresses were spread on the floor, there wasn't much extra room. They picked ants from their food and lice from their hair. A bath meant dunking in frigid water. Their toilet served more than forty prisoners. On some days, they could hear blood-curdling screams from nearby cells; at other times, they watched as other women prisoners were savagely beaten.

To a casual observer, the prospects for the women's release looked bleak, especially after the United States began bombing Taliban strongholds on October 7. But the Waco church continued its twenty-four-hour-a-day praying, using a web site to mobilize the entire nation to pray for the two women. Pastor Seibert called prayer "the key to unlocking the Taliban's prison doors." He said he expected a miracle like the one in Acts 12, when Peter was released from prison in Jerusalem by an angel.

15

Never be afraid to trust an unknown future to a known God.

Corrie ten Boom

Due to prayer and politics, Curry and Mercer were treated rather well, despite the difficult conditions. As a U.S. State Department official commented, "They were high profile—the whole world was watching." But regardless of international pressure, the two were in a war zone.

When the American bombs struck Kabul, the prison walls shook. "Our prison was shaking," Mercer said. "All we could do was sit and pray." And pray they did—for three hours a day. Of course, they prayed for themselves, but they prayed mostly for the Afghan people whom they had come to love.

God had them in the Kabul jail for a purpose, they believed, and that was to raise prayer for the people and nation of Afghanistan. If their imprisonment accomplished that, they said, "it has all been worth it."

On the night of November 12, Taliban soldiers burst into their cells and ordered them to pack up. The women grabbed what they could before being herded into a van. "We were stepping on rocket launchers," said Curry, "plus I had this Afghan guard with a gun next to me. It was probably the first time I really, really felt we were in danger."

The Taliban were fleeing in panic. Mercer and Curry could see other soldiers fleeing too. Then Mercer pulled out a Bible and began reading Scriptures. Soon the whole group of prisoners was singing and laughing. "It was really the presence of God there," she said.

After they rode toward Kandahar for several hours, the van stopped suddenly, and the prisoners were ordered to enter a metal shipping container. They spent the night with twenty armed Taliban soldiers guarding them. Early the next morning, the jail door opened . . . and an opposition commander stood there, telling the women, "You're free, you're free, you're free." The next moments were chaotic. Curry and Mercer had to set their head coverings on fire to show a rescue helicopter where to land. But soon they were picked up and transported to a safer place. Eventually they were reunited with loved ones and with the church that, throughout the ordeal, had upheld them in prayer.

Oklahoma City

"I Couldn't Outrun Prayer"

Sergeant Arlene Blanchard had nine days left in the military. In fact, April 19, 1995, was her last day as an army personnel sergeant in Oklahoma City. On this day she was so invigorated that, instead of taking the elevator, she ran up the stairs to her fourth-floor office in the Murrah federal office building. There she met the sergeant who would replace her, along with his wife and two little daughters. After the introductions, she excused herself to finish some reports.

Then, she says, it "seemed like a ton of bricks hit me in the center of my head, and volts of electricity shot up the tips of my toes and coursed through my body and out the top of my head. My entire body was vibrating and shaking. I was plunged into total darkness and began screaming at the top of my lungs."

This wasn't the first calamity in Arlene Blanchard's life. She had already had more than her share of trouble. Raised in one of Cleveland's housing projects, as a child she often went to bed hungry. Sometimes she wished she had never been born. Surrounded by violence, she quickly learned how to protect herself. One of her dreams was to be a walking lethal weapon, maybe even an assassin.

After joining the army, Arlene spent time in Italy and then was stationed in Alaska. It was a tough place to live, so she spent her time drinking and carousing. One morning after a wild weekend, she looked at herself in the mirror and was shocked to see the person she had become.

At that low point, she remembered her praying mother. "I soon learned that no matter how hard I ran, I couldn't outrun prayer," she said later. On a cold and dismal day in Alaska, she

They [the Israelites] said to Samuel, "Do not stop crying out to the LORD our God for us, that he may rescue us from the hand of the Philistines."

1 Samuel 7:8

found a little church. "I couldn't resist God's love any longer." She invited Christ into her life.

Then came Oklahoma City, 1995. The explosion, the total darkness, the screaming. Arlene was unconscious for five minutes. When she regained her sight, she tried to run toward an exit, but found nowhere to go. The entire office had been demolished. Just to her left was an opening later known as "the pit." Nine floors of the building were stacked one on top of another, like pancakes.

She screamed again. The thought crossed her mind that she should be able to handle this. After all, she had been trained in the army to keep calm in all types of circumstances. But she couldn't handle this and she knew it.

Instinctively she thrust her arms toward heaven and cried, "Jesus, my Jesus." She just wanted Jesus to hold her hand. And he did. She says, "Right then, before I had even finished saying his name, his loving peace covered me like a soft, downy blanket, and immediately I stopped screaming. What I remember most about that day is that Jesus was the first one there to hold my hand."

About thirty minutes later, Arlene and some of the fourth-floor survivors walked out of the building.

The horror of that experience left its mark. Arlene had stomach ulcers, chronic migraines, and night after night of sleeplessness as a result. Even her appearance was changed. "At twenty-eight," she says, "I could have passed for Methuselah's grandmother."

One hundred sixty-eight people died as a result of the bombing. Many others were scarred both physically and emotionally. But thanks to the one who held her hand, Arlene Blanchard lived through the bombing to tell about it. In the aftermath, she and her husband, Stan, began a ministry called The Cross and the Dove to help people triumph through tragedy in their lives. No one can doubt her credentials.

East Germany

Why the Wall Came Tumbling Down

The East Germans called it *Die Wende,* the "turning point." It happened on October 9, 1989, in Leipzig, a bastion of the Protestant Reformation. Perhaps it was appropriate that these world-changing events occurred in a city where Luther had reformed religion in the sixteenth century and Bach had reformed music in the eighteenth.

Throughout the 1980s, four churches in Leipzig (including Bach's old church) were holding weekly prayer meetings every Monday evening at five o'clock. The pastors led the old Lutheran hymns, addressed their congregations with the Bible in one hand, and began rounds of prayer. For most of that decade, a handful of Christians, a few dozen at most, would assemble for these prayer meetings. But change was brewing in 1989, and that's when the attendance began to swell. Philip Yancey tells the story in his book *Finding God in Unexpected Places.*

The church was the one place where the Communist state allowed freedom of assembly. So these prayer meetings began to attract not only faithful Christians but also political dissidents and curious citizens. After each Monday evening meeting, the groups began to join together and walk through the dark streets of the old city holding candles and banners—a most benign form of political protest.

Eventually news media from the West picked up the story. Alarmed, the Communist hierarchy debated how to stamp out the peaceful marches. Secret police surrounded the churches, sometimes roughing up the marchers. But the crowds in Leipzig kept growing: hundreds, thousands, eventually fifty thousand.

On October 9, the "turning point," the East German government stepped in. Police and army units moved into Leipzig in force, and East German leader Erich Honecker gave the instructions to shoot the demonstrators. The country braced for a disaster. Leipzig's Lutheran bishop warned of a massacre, hospitals cleared emergency rooms, and churches and concert halls agreed to open their doors in case demonstrators needed quick refuge.

When the time came for the prayer meeting at Nikolai Church, two thousand Communist Party members rushed inside to occupy all the seats. The church simply opened its seldom-used balconies, and a thousand protestors crowded into them.

No one knows for sure why the soldiers held their fire that night. But everyone credits the prayer vigils in Leipzig for kindling the process of momentous change. That night 70,000 people marched peacefully through downtown Leipzig. The following Monday, 120,000 marched. A week later, 500,000 turned out—nearly the entire population of Leipzig.

In early November, the largest march of all took place, almost one million people marching peacefully, now through East Berlin, the capital. Erich Honecker resigned, humiliated. Police disobeyed orders to fire on the demonstrators. And at midnight on November 9, something happened that few had even dared to pray for—a gap opened up in the hated Berlin Wall. East Germans streamed through the checkpoints, past guards who had always followed orders to "shoot to kill." Not a single life was lost as throngs of people marching with candles brought down a government.

Within a few months, the peaceful revolution spread across the globe. Ten nations comprising more than half a billion people—Poland, East Germany, Hungary, Czechoslovakia, Bulgaria, Romania, Albania, Yugoslavia, Mongolia, the Soviet Union—experienced nonviolent revolutions.

As Bud Bultman, a producer and writer for CNN, wrote: "We in the media watched in astonishment as the walls of totalitarianism came crashing down. But in the rush to cover the cataclysmic events, the story behind the story was overlooked. We trained our cameras on hundreds of thousands of people praying for freedom, votive candles in hand, and yet we missed the transcendent dimension, the explicitly spiritual and religious character of the story. We looked right at it and could not see it."

20

Some did see it. East Germans still speak of those days as a miracle. The *New Republic* reported, "Whether or not prayers really move mountains, they certainly mobilized the population of Leipzig. To hear them sing 'A Mighty Fortress Is Our God' is enough to make you believe it."

Several weeks after the October 9 turning point, a huge banner appeared across a Leipzig street: *Wir danken Dir, Kirche*— "We thank you, church."

Beirut

"It Was Just God and Me"

The date: May 8, 1984. The place: Beirut, Lebanon. Ben and Carol Weir had just left their apartment and were now walking to the Near East School of Theology, where they worked. A car stopped. Two men got out, grabbed Ben, and shoved him into the car. Carol screamed, but no one seemed to pay attention. In the car a man with a black beard pointed a pistol at Ben's head. The driver pulled away as Ben was forced to the floor of the back seat, a sack placed over his head.

Ben sized up his situation: "I was a captive and saw no way to escape. I didn't trust these men. I believed them to be dangerous and unpredictable. But I had one important resource they could not touch: faith in the living God."

On Ben's first night in captivity, a guard told him to face the wall and take off his blindfold. Ben was given a pair of ski goggles with the eyeholes covered with thick adhesive tape. The guard checked to see that the headband was tight. "Good," said the guard. "No see." Weir was in total darkness. He described himself as "vulnerable, lonely, and helpless."

When the guard left him, Weir remembered the Bible verse from the Gospel of John: "If ye abide in me and my words abide in you, ye shall ask what ye will, and it shall be done unto you" (John 15:7 KJV). Then he prayed, "Lord, I remember your promise, and I think it applies to me too. . . . I'm in need. I need you.

The king's heart is in the hand of the LORD;
he directs it like a watercourse wherever he pleases.

Proverbs 21:1

I need your assurance and guidance to be faithful to you in this situation. . . . Deliver me from this place and this captivity if it is your will."

Ben had plenty of time to pray, and in the early days of his captivity he prayed repeatedly, "Lord, here I am. You know where I am, even if I do not. You know how I came here and what's going to happen. You know who my captors are, even if I do not. I'm helpless. I'm in your hands. Help me to trust you."

Weir says he was completely dependent on God. "It was just God and me without any cushion in between." He did physical exercises by counting, "One, two, three, hallelujah, five, six, seven, praise the Lord."

During the next sixteen months, Weir was moved repeatedly, was threatened often, had a gun held to the back of his neck, and was told that the building in which he was held might be detonated. He also was placed with other captives, and their captors loved to torment them all. Once, a guard told Weir he deserved to be killed and put a pistol against his cheek. Occasionally one of the guards would come into his room, cock his pistol, and pull the trigger on an empty chamber.

Ben was finally allowed to have a New Testament and later a whole Bible. One story that he read often was about the persistent widow who knocked and knocked at the judge's door until the judge finally responded. Ben felt he was praying to God just as persistently as that widow had beseeched the judge.

Then suddenly in September 1985, sixteen months after he had been kidnapped, the chief of the guards announced that Benjamin Weir had been selected as the captive to be released. At first Weir and the other captives did not think their captor was serious. But soon he was taken out to a car and ordered to lie facedown on the back seat. After a twenty-minute ride, the car stopped. Weir was allowed to get out and take off his face mask as the car sped away. It was near midnight, but he recognized the area, and he found his way to a friend's house. The next day he was in the American Embassy and free again. God had delivered him.

Pearl Harbor

"Father, Forgive Them"

The conversion of Mitsuo Fuchida was certainly an answer to prayer. But whose prayer?

Commander Mitsuo Fuchida was the lead pilot of the 360 planes that bombed Pearl Harbor on December 7, 1941. He was the one who gave the order to attack, shouting the code words "Tora, Tora, Tora!" A fearless pilot whose dive-bombing skills were legendary, he had racked up more flying hours than any other Japanese pilot. As a national hero, he was even granted an audience with Emperor Hirohito.

But by August 1945, things were not going well for the Japanese forces. Fuchida was on duty in Hiroshima when he was summoned to army headquarters. He left the city late in the afternoon. The next day, the first atomic bomb leveled the city he had just left.

After the war, as he spoke to a friend who had been captured by the United States, Fuchida was surprised at how well Japanese prisoners had been treated. His friend told of a volunteer, Peggy Covell, who was especially kind and courteous. When one Japanese prisoner had asked her why she was being so gracious, she told him, "Because Japanese soldiers killed my parents." Her parents, missionary teachers in Japan before the war, had fled to the Philippines, where they were captured and judged to be spies. They were beheaded while kneeling in prayer.

In America, Peggy received word of her parents' fate. When she thought of how they died, she was filled with hate. Killed while praying! But then she began wondering what they were praying about. No doubt they were praying for the Japanese, asking God to forgive them. Peggy felt that God was asking her

23

to forgive the Japanese also and to demonstrate her forgiveness by serving them.

Fuchida was astounded by the story. Not long afterward, while waiting at a railroad station in Tokyo, he was given a tract written by an American pilot, Jacob DeShazor, who had been captured by the Japanese and imprisoned for forty months, mostly in solitary confinement. The tract told how this American pilot had hated the Japanese because of the treatment he had received while imprisoned. But in prison he read the Bible and was converted. "Love your enemies" had been a hard command for DeShazor, but soon he began praying for the Japanese. The tract said that the pilot planned to return to Japan as a missionary to share the love of Christ.

Again Fuchida was astounded. He decided to buy a Bible for himself. Although he didn't read it for several months, eventually he saw the words of Jesus Christ, "Father, forgive them, for they know not what they do." Not only had Peggy Covell's parents, Peggy Covell herself, and the American pilot included him in their prayers as they were praying for the Japanese people—now it seemed that Jesus himself was praying for him as he died on the cross!

Fuchida burst out in tears. Within a year, he accepted Christ as his Savior. Soon he met the American pilot DeShazor, and over the next few years, the two of them spoke to large crowds in the United States and Japan. Thousands were won to Christ.

There's no denying that Fuchida was converted as an answer to prayer, but *whose* prayer doesn't really matter, does it?

Moscow

"What a God We've Got"

"God does not answer prayer," Jerome Hines said when he was twenty-one. "He is not a personal deity who busies himself with the mundane affairs of two billion individuals." A promising young opera singer, Hines had never had a prayer answered or seen anything that came close to being a miracle.

Three years later he signed a contract to sing at the Metropolitan Opera in New York. Soon he won the coveted Caruso Award, given to the outstanding young Met singer of the year. In 1950 he sang on network television and played Mephistopheles in *Faust* three times at the Hollywood Bowl. Success was sweet for Jerome Hines.

Though he was not a Christian, Hines liked the Sermon on the Mount and considered putting it to music. He also wanted to create an operatic passion play. But to do all that, he had to read the Bible.

One night in a dream, he saw a black book opened up beside him. Two lines were illuminated, and as he began to read he heard a voice from heaven reading along with him: "This is my beloved Son, in whom I am well pleased" (Matt. 3:17 KJV).

When he awoke, he couldn't forget his dream. A twofold message struck him: Not only was Jesus the Son of God, but he, Jerome Hines, was not a son of God. "I saw Jerome Hines there as a grain of dust," he recalled later. Gradually Hines was led into a personal relationship with Jesus Christ, and the opera star who didn't believe in a personal God and didn't believe in prayer was now talking to God regularly and experiencing miracles in his own life.

At the height of his career in the early 1960s, Jerome Hines was invited to Russia to sing *Faust* and *Boris Gudonov* at the famed Bolshoi Opera. This was at the peak of the Cold War. The United States and the USSR were enemies but occasionally had cultural exchanges. Hines's performances were so well received that he was asked to extend his visit. At times fatigue and a bad throat threatened to make him cancel, but each time the Lord restored him in time for the next concert. Then as he returned to Moscow for a final concert, he prayed, "Lord, do your servant just one more favor. Give me Khrushchev at my return performance at the Bolshoi." Nikita Khrushchev was the Russian premier.

It was impossible, Hines's manager said. The international situation was too tense. Khrushchev wouldn't think of coming, even if he wanted to. But Hines prayed anyway.

At breakfast on the morning of the performance, Hines heard the news that President Kennedy had announced a blockade of Cuba. "They'll be stopping any Russian ships that try to run the blockade," he was told. "This could mean war."

It also meant that his Russian audience that night might be hostile. As for Khrushchev, forget about it. But Hines had a personal relationship with a miracle-working God, and he kept praying for a miracle.

And just before the curtain opened, Hines heard, "Khrushchev's coming! Khrushchev's coming!"

Hines responded, "What a God we've got! What a God we've got!"

After the performance, Hines and his wife, Lucia, were welcomed by Khrushchev and about thirty Communist leaders. In his best Russian, the American opera star told the Russian premier, "God bless you."

Jerome and Lucia Hines returned to the United States as the only Americans to see the Russian leader during those crucial days. Hines said, "We were a small part of one of the great climaxes of history." Indeed, the world was poised for war. Kennedy and Khrushchev were both talking tough as Russian ships loaded with missiles cruised toward Cuba. But not long after he met the Christian opera singer, Khrushchev made his remarkable decision to pull back from the brink of war.

Miracles big and small. Peace grabbed from the jaws of conflict. A surprise guest at a musical event. And a once-skeptical singer who, as he puts it, "found that miracles exist and that God is a personal God who cares for the individual—in fact, he cared enough to die for me."

"Pray for the Miners"

Late in July 2002, in the Quecreek Mine near Somerset, Pennsylvania, nine miners broke through a wall to an abandoned mine filled with decades of storm water runoff. Maps showed the abandoned mine three hundred feet away from the miners' location, but something was wrong. As soon as the miners' machinery penetrated that wall, a torrent burst in on them— an estimated sixty million gallons of frigid water, the equivalent of seventy Olympic-size swimming pools.

Now these nine men found themselves trapped 240 feet underground, and the water was rising. Only twice in modern history had miners been trapped by water like this, and both times there had been no survivors. And as if that picture weren't bleak enough, this occurred only ten miles from the site of the survivorless crash of United Flight 93 on September 11, 2001.

The miners sought to find the highest ground in the mine, but they were no match for the surging water. Mark Popernack, a twenty-two-year coal-mining veteran, had been running the drill that caused the breach. Now he was separated from the others by a wall of water too powerful to cross. With thoughts of imminent death, he could only pray. And pray he did, harder than he had ever prayed in his life. After two hours of those lonely prayers, the water receded enough for his comrades to reach him with the scoop of a mining lift. Mark climbed in and rode across to join the others. He considered that mini-rescue an answer to prayer, but there were many troubles yet to come, and many more prayers.

Up on the surface, a sign went up at the local Wendy's: "Pray for the Miners." In fact, throughout Somerset County, signs on restaurants, gas stations, homes, and street corners urged people to pray.

At the mine, engineers were working furiously to save the miners. First, they tried to punch a six-inch pipe into the mine, providing fresh air from the surface. As it happened, the pipe reached the exact location where the miners were stranded just as they were about to run out of breath. Some of the miners called it their first answer to prayer. There were more to come.

The air from the pipe caused pressure that pushed the water level down. Now drowning was less likely, but if they weren't discovered soon, they might starve to death. Then the miners saw a lunch pail floating by. One of them had brought it to work that day and set it down somewhere, but now this subterranean river had carried it to them just when they needed it most. The pail contained a corned beef sandwich and a can of Mountain Dew. Each of the nine men took a bite of the sandwich and a sip or two of the soda. It was miracle number two.

The third miracle was one they didn't recognize until later. In fact, it seemed like very bad news at the time. They had been taking comfort from the sound of drilling from up above, but now the drilling stopped. Why? What had gone wrong?

Above ground, frustrated engineers told the public that a fifteen-hundred-pound drill bit had broken in the escape tunnel, and now they would have to get a new drill bit and start over again. It delayed the rescue fifteen hours. By now this was national news. Around the country and around the world, people were praying for the miners. But this delay was a confusing setback.

Later, Governor Mark Schweiker of Pennsylvania called the broken drill bit a case of "providential intervention." If the shaft had broken through where they were drilling, it would have caused even more flooding, drowning the miners. Instead, the delay allowed the engineers to pump out water, twenty thousand gallons a minute. Meanwhile, the engineers turned their attention to a second site for drilling, based on "blind hope and an informed guess." A state official said, "Those guys could have been anywhere in a square mile down there." They had to hit the right spot "on the money," he said. And they did. A safety expert called it "unprecedented."

After seventy-seven hours, the drill at the second location broke into the chamber 240 feet underground. The first response the engineers heard from the miners was, "Praise the Lord." The last to come up was Mark Popernack, who had been praying for a miracle since the whole thing started. Then Governor Schweiker announced to the world, "Nine for nine." All miners were alive and well.

A sign in Andrea's Restaurant said simply, "Thank you, Lord." At Mel's Restaurant the owner said, "We went from feeling somebody slapped us to knowing that our prayers are answered." One Somerset resident remarked, "The mines can be hell, but there are miracles that can happen too."

Throughout Pennsylvania, the nation, and the world, people praised God for the safe return of the nine miners. Many applauded the tireless efforts of the rescuers and the tenacity of the miners, but as *USA Today* commented, "More than a few credited divine intervention."

Cape Town

The End of Apartheid

"It's going to be a bloodbath." That's what political observers around the world were saying when South African apartheid collapsed in the early 1990s. The white regime that had maintained an oppressive separation of the races was stepping down. A black leader, Nelson Mandela, was elected president. Watchers feared that the long-oppressed races would use violence to gain vengeance.

The bloodbath never happened, however, and newspapers used the word *miraculous* to describe the peaceful transition.

Why did it turn out like this? In a word—prayer.

The newspapers praised Mandela, and certainly his handling of the delicate transfer of power was remarkable. But two other men, men of prayer, had been working and praying behind the scenes for years.

Desmond Tutu had already been awarded the Nobel Peace Prize in 1984 and then had been named the first black archbishop of Cape Town in 1986. He walked a political tightrope, calling for an end to apartheid on one hand and opposing violence on the other. One biographer states, "Simultaneously loved and hated, honored and vilified, Tutu became a key figure in one of the most notorious confrontations between Church and State in the history of Christianity."

As a young man, Tutu got into the habit of beginning each day at 5:30 (or earlier) with prayer before his morning jog. Without it, he said, "I feel a physical discomfort—it is worse than having forgotten to brush my teeth! . . . I would be completely rudderless . . . if I did not have these times with God."

Our God has boundless resources. The only limit is in us. Our asking, our thinking, our praying are too small. Our expectations are too limited.

A. B. Simpson

One time after police roughed him up and threatened to kill him, he thanked God for keeping him safe. Later he said, "The most awful thing they can do is to kill me, and death is not the worst thing that can happen to a Christian."

He denounced violence, whether it came from the white-dominated government or from his fellow blacks. At the funeral of a South African black activist who was brutally killed by security police, Tutu told the restless crowd, "I bid you pray for the rulers of this land, for the police, especially the security police and those in the prison service, that they may realize that they are human beings too. I bid you pray for whites in South Africa."

Looking ahead prophetically in 1980 to the time when apartheid would be overthrown, Tutu said, "We need Nelson Mandela," even though Mandela was serving a life sentence in prison at the time. It was Tutu who not only kept blacks from boiling over but also influenced his friend Mandela to say at his inaugural, "We enter into a covenant that we shall build the society in which all South Africans, both black and white, will be able to walk tall."

Also significant was the role played by Michael Cassidy, a white South African who was the international team leader of African Enterprise. Beginning in April 1993, Cassidy organized more than a thousand groups to pray in round-the-clock prayer chain vigils for the election. In one large prayer rally, a key black political leader who had threatened to boycott the election changed his mind. The newspapers called it a major breakthrough. Then shortly before the election, Cassidy organized a "Jesus peace rally" to seek the will of the Lord in South Africa. Some thirty thousand people joined in the interracial event. The influence of that rally went far beyond the thousands who attended.

For weeks after the election and the inauguration of Nelson Mandela, secular reporters called it a miracle. What the reporters didn't see was the church on its knees.

3

Surprise, Surprise

When God Does the Unexpected

"I tell you the truth, if anyone says to this mountain, 'Go throw yourself into the sea,' and does not doubt in his heart but believes that what he says will happen, it will be done for him. Therefore, I tell you, whatever you ask for in prayer, believe that you have received it, and it will be yours."

Mark 11:23–24

God keeps us guessing. Just when we think we know everything about his *modus operandi*, he stuns us with something new. When the apostle talked about God doing more than we can ask or even imagine, he was on target. That's one thing we can count on: God is a God of surprises.

Sometimes he surprises us by answering those desperation prayers we don't really expect to be answered. We all have those moments of crying, "Lord, get me out of this mess!" Sometimes that's exactly what happens.

Sometimes God surprises us by answering the trivial prayers we pray. A parking place. The right color shoes. A teenage romance. Why should the ruler of the universe bother with these matters? Yet he does.

Most often, God surprises us with the *way* he answers our prayers. We sometimes try to figure out the precise scenario of God's workings, and we're usually way off. Yet God finds other ways to fulfill our wants and needs—better ways.

> *Loving God, in your hand, my lopsided life is being transformed into vibrant symmetry.*

> Carol Knapp

Moving a Mountain by Faith

It was called Sunrise Home, which might have been appropriate if it weren't for a mountain that blocked the sun for much of the day. Still, in the 1930s it was a place of new opportunity for orphaned Japanese girls, many of whom would otherwise be destined for brothels.

One day a mother came with her four children, the youngest a baby with tuberculosis. Her husband had been killed in an earthquake, which had also destroyed their home and all their possessions. Sunrise Home wasn't really designed for families, but Irene Webster-Smith, the missionary who ran the place, made an exception, taking in this needy bunch. It was obvious, however, that the baby needed medical attention, so he was taken away to a sanitarium.

Over the following weeks, the baby seemed to get weaker and weaker. The doctor at the sanitarium wanted to reunite the child with the mother. Besides, the fresh air at the Sunrise Home would be good for the baby—but the baby also needed sunlight, and the mountain was in the way. Webster-Smith wondered if there was any way she could get rid of that mountain.

Back at Sunrise Home, she told the other children the predicament, and they wanted to help. "I know what we can do," one said. "We can take away the mountain ourselves, one shovelful of dirt at a time." So everyone pitched in, but their little shovels hardly dented the mountain. It seemed as huge as ever.

Heavenly Father, you opened my eyes to see letting go is making room for Your gifts to enter.

Oscar Green

One day Webster-Smith was asked to travel to another Japanese city to meet with the head of her mission. The children said they would continue shoveling in her absence. Almost as an afterthought, Webster-Smith suggested they pray about the mountain before she left. Some of the prayers were discouraging, and then one girl prayed, "Lord Jesus, last Sunday we heard in Sunday school that if we had faith as a grain of mustard seed, we could remove mountains. Lord, help us remove our mountain." Another prayed, "Dear Lord, you said we could move a mountain into the sea. Here the sea is just across the road. Will you please take our mountain and put it into the sea?"

Webster-Smith's meeting with the mission director lasted longer than she had expected. Then one day she received a card from the children of Sunrise Home. "When are you coming home?" it said. "Hurry. We have a wonderful surprise for you."

When she returned, they led her in the back way and told her not to peek. Then they brought her to the front yard and said, "Look!"

She looked. The mountain was gone; it was nowhere in sight. She couldn't believe it. "What happened?" she asked.

The children were so excited that their words tumbled on top of one another. The preceding week, a truck filled with workers had come up the hill. Without a word, the workers swarmed over the mountain with pickaxes and shovels, loading the dirt onto the truck. Truckload after truckload was carted away. Finally one of the assistants at Sunrise Home asked what was going on, and the supervisor explained that they needed to fill in some land to make a children's playground where the sea had receded, so this "mountain" was being used for fill.

"The Lord really did answer our prayers," explained one little girl to her teacher.

As so often happens, God provided even more. Not only did the Lord move the mountain, as the girls requested, but he also provided them with a playground.

And the following week, the little baby with tuberculosis was reunited with his mother in the sunbathed Sunrise Home.

Rhoda's Big Surprise

It's A.D. 43. A prisoner is chained to two soldiers in the tower of Antonia at the northwest corner of the temple in Jerusalem; two more soldiers are guarding the doors. Who is this fearsome threat to society? A murderer? A terrorist? No, it's Simon Peter, a leader of the people who worship Jesus of Nazareth.

Maybe a half mile southwest of the temple complex, a group of those Jesus followers meets in an upper room at the home of a woman named Mary and her son John Mark. Are they plotting to overthrow the oppressive government? No, they're praying. They're asking God to arrange for Peter's release.

Not long before this, King Herod Agrippa had beheaded James, one of Jesus' closest disciples. It was a great blow to the young Christian community to lose this leader—no doubt what Herod intended. Then he had arrested Peter, the next Christian leader on his hit list. If it weren't Passover week, Peter would have been executed already. Instead, he is confined to the tower of Antonia with four guards on duty at all times.

The home of Mary and Mark is probably the usual meeting place for the Christians, ever since Jesus celebrated his last Passover there with his disciples thirteen years earlier. The Jesus movement had erupted at Pentecost, when the Holy Spirit descended upon the disciples, but the fervor of those early days now has diminished somewhat. The execution of James has surely shaken them, and now they're desperately praying for a miracle to spring Peter.

Meanwhile, something strange is happening at the tower of Antonia. Peter is sleeping soundly; maybe his guards are sleeping too, but with Peter chained to them there's no chance for escape. Suddenly an angel of the Lord appears, shines a light in Peter's face, taps him on the shoulder, and says, in effect, "Let's go, and make it quick." Before Peter has a chance to think about the chains or to protest how absurdly impossible this sounds, the chains fall off. The angel leads him past the guards and out of jail.

New mercies, each
returning day,
Hover around us
while we pray;
New perils past,
new sins forgiven,
New thoughts of
God, new hopes
of heaven.

John Keble

Peter has no idea that this is really happening; it has to be a dream. He walks out of the tower toward the iron gate leading to the city, and his freedom still seems surreal. The gate opens, and the angel walks Peter down one street and then disappears. Alone in Jerusalem's dark city streets, Peter finally realizes he's not dreaming. As soon as he gets his bearings, he heads straight to the upper room, where he knows he'll find a group of disciples.

The entrance gate to the courtyard of Mary's home is locked, so Peter knocks on it. A servant girl, Rhoda, comes to answer it. "Who's there?"

"It's me, Peter."

Rhoda can't believe it. That's just what they were praying for, and here he is. She rushes to tell the others—but in her excitement she neglects to open the gate for Peter to come in. The escaped convict is left standing there, still knocking.

"Peter is at the door!" Rhoda tells the praying disciples.

"You're out of your mind," they answer. Maybe she saw an angel or something. But there's that knocking sound again. Why would an angel have to knock? Others go out to the gate to see for themselves. There stands the answer to their prayers—Peter, unchained.

It's an amazing story of answered prayer, amazing not just because of God's miraculous answer, but also because God surprised everyone. Peter thought he was dreaming, Rhoda was completely befuddled, and the praying disciples thought Rhoda

A Christian on his knees sees more than the philosopher on tiptoes.

Anonymous

was seeing things. Yet no matter how meager their faith, the power of God was strong enough to break all chains.

Prayer Answers by the Bunch

In a disease-ridden concentration camp during World War II, Darlene Deibler found her faith severely tested and surprisingly strengthened. She and her husband, Russell, were working as missionaries in New Guinea when they were captured by the Japanese. He died in the prison camp. She became quite ill but lived to tell about it in her autobiography, *Evidence Not Seen*.

She often found worms and insects swimming around in her soup. Though she was repulsed, she knew she had to eat. So she learned to crush the worms and insects in her fingers and eat them with her soup. She developed severe dysentery and diarrhea, and the Epsom salts and quinine she received did no good. She also seemed to be suffering from malaria and beriberi. Finally she prayed, "Lord, I'm being constantly reinfected by these flies, so if it please you, heal me."

After praying, she felt that the Lord would heal her as she had requested, so she refused her daily doses of Epsom salts and quinine. All symptoms left her.

Sometime later, as she looked out the window of her cell, she saw a person with some bananas in the distance. She began to crave a banana, even just a bite. She could smell the bananas and almost taste them. The craving grew unbearable. Dropping to her knees, she prayed, "Lord, I'm not asking you for a whole bunch. . . . I just want one banana, Lord, just one banana."

Then she realized how foolish it was to pray such a thing. How could God possibly get a banana to her through the prison walls? "There was more of a chance of the moon falling out of the sky than of one of the [guards] bringing me a banana," she realized. Bowing her head again, she prayed, "Lord, there's no one here who could get a banana to me. There's no way for you to do it. Please don't think I'm not

36

thankful for the rice porridge. It's just that—well, those bananas looked so delicious!"

In *Real Stories for the Soul,* Robert J. Morgan tells how the Lord answered Darlene's prayer:

> The next morning, she heard the guard coming down the concrete walkway. The door opened, and it was the warden of the POW camp who had taken kindly to her. He looked down at her emaciated body and, without saying a word, turned and left, locking the door behind him. Sometime later, she heard another set of footsteps and the door opened. The guard threw a huge yellow bundle into the cell, saying, "They're yours!" She counted them. It was a bundle of ninety-two bananas!
>
> As she began peeling her bananas, Ephesians 3:20 came to her mind: *God is able to do exceedingly, abundantly above all that we can ask or think, according to the power that works in us.*
>
> She never again read that verse without thinking of bananas.

Indeed, God's answers sometimes come in bunches.

Russian Room Service

The Soviet Lausanne Congress in October 1990 was miraculous in many ways. Who would have thought—even a few years earlier—that you could bring thirteen hundred Christian leaders from all over Russia to plan the evangelization of the Soviet Union? Many things were beginning to change at that time. Within the next year, the Soviet Union would suddenly cease to exist.

John Robb, who worked for a division of World Vision International, was directing a seminar at the convention. His subject: how to win Muslims for Christ. To his surprise, Robb discovered that one man who had been helping him work out arrangements with the Russian-speaking hotel staff was a Muslim himself. Even more surprising, this man asked if he could attend Robb's seminar. Absolutely!

He answered prayer:
  so sweetly that I
  stand
Amid the blessing of
  His wondrous hand
And marvel at the
  miracle I see,
The favors that His
  love hath wrought
  for me.
Pray on for the
  impossible, and dare
Upon thy banner this
  brave motto bear,
"My Father answers
  prayer."
  Rosalind Goforth

Afterward, when John Robb was preparing to check out of his hotel room, this Muslim man knocked on his door. He had come to say good-bye, handing Robb some books about Russia as well as his business card. Robb looked around his room for something to give in return, but he had already given away all the Christian literature he had brought.

John prayed silently for something to give: *A Russian New Testament would be ideal, Lord.* The thought seemed ridiculous. The nation had been closed to Christianity for so long, you'd never expect to find a New Testament lying around. But Robb had hardly finished his one-sentence prayer when another knock came at the door.

Outside stood two Russian men next to a cart piled high with books. The books were New Testaments—Russian New Testaments. Robb's mouth fell open. Were these men angels? What were they doing there with a cartful of New Testaments?

"We're Gideons," one of them explained, "putting Bibles in the rooms of this hotel." A month earlier, they said, Soviet president Mikhail Gorbachev had approved a law lifting restrictions on freedom of religion. "We've just received permission to distribute New Testaments to every room in this hotel." Robb thanked them profusely, took a copy, and presented it as a gift to his Muslim friend.

Three months later, he received a letter from the man. "This book," he wrote, "is my friend and constant companion. I've read it and reread it." And when John Robb returned to Russia eight months later, he looked up this old friend. Over dinner at a Moscow restaurant, the man quietly said, "I have given my heart to Jesus Christ as my Savior. I've put my faith in him."

The world was amazed at the rapid fall of the Soviet empire in 1991. Christians around the world were thrilled at the new openness in those lands to the message of Christ. John Robb is still stunned that these world trends converged one afternoon in a Russian hotel room when he needed a gift for a curious friend.

When God Healed a Windmill

In the desert region of northwestern Kenya, water is liquid gold. In some areas, windmills pump water from underground and thus are vital to the people of those areas.

The nomadic Turkana people relied on one such windmill near the little settlement of Lorengalup. It usually pumped about 625 gallons of groundwater per day, enough for almost a hundred people plus two or three herds of goats or camels. The Turkana women hauled water from the windmill to their huts every day in plastic jerricans atop their heads. The problem was, the windmill's pump kept breaking down.

Missionaries Randy and Edie Nelson had served in that area for nine years and had spent much of that time fixing the windmill, always managing to get it up and spinning again. But in the early fall of 1989, the Turkana women noticed the water level dropping in the covered cement tank next to the windmill. Water normally flowed up from the 125-foot pump shaft through a length of two-inch galvanized pipe into the storage tank. But when Randy took the lid off the tank, he saw a mere trickle dribbling from the pipe. Then the water stopped completely.

Randy radioed missionary colleague Bob Chapman to come help replace the suction-cup gaskets inside the pump, a procedure they had performed several times before. But this failed to solve the problem. They tried other ideas; nothing worked. Time to call in extra help and equipment.

Randy radioed Mike Harris, the Kenyan contractor who had built the windmill in 1980. With a mechanic at his side, Mike flew to Lorengalup in his small plane, bringing along a large hand-driven winch to solve the problem. Now four men were working on the pump, but eventually Mike concluded, "The whole pump will have to be replaced," and he agreed to get a new one.

Randy and Bob put the broken pump back in place so they would know exactly how to piece it all together when the new pump arrived. Then they waited. Two days later Mike called, saying he couldn't locate a new pump, so the Nelsons drove to Nairobi to see what they could find there. Before Randy left, he climbed the thirty-foot-tall metal support frame of the windmill to shut down the fiberglass blade. More damage could result if the mechanism continued to pump dry.

Randy scouted everywhere in Nairobi without success. Finally he ordered a pump from the United States, though he knew it would take a long time to arrive. He resigned himself to the thought that the Turkana people would be without water for a while.

When the Nelsons returned to Lorengalup, however, Randy saw that the windmill blades were spinning. He was disturbed. *Some kids must have been fiddling with the chain that shuts down the blades*, he thought.

As they approached their home, a young man ran up, shouting, "The windmill—it's pumping water again!"

The Nelsons were skeptical, but the young man continued, "A couple days after you left, about a dozen women decided to pray for the windmill, just as you've been teaching us to pray for the sick. They figured if God can heal bodies, why not a broken windmill?"

In fact, the young man told them, a group of Turkana women had surrounded the windmill, laid their hands on it, and prayed for its repair. Within two hours, a strong wind arose and struck the windmill squarely. Somehow the metal chain broke, the tail unfolded into the wind, and the blades began to twirl with abandon. Someone went to check the water storage tank and discovered fresh water now pouring out of the pipe. The women praised God for his dramatic answer to their prayers of faith.

Randy went to the windmill to see for himself. He couldn't understand how a broken pump that did not seal could possibly pull water out of the ground. But the windmill continued pumping water. When the new pump arrived from the States, the flow of the old pump stopped.

Today the region hosts well over a thousand nomadic Turkana believers, most of whom have heard how the God who rules the universe has no trouble healing a windmill.

The Mysterious Phone Booth

Same old, same old. Ken Gaub of Yakima, Washington, was at a crossroads in his Christian life and ministry. Part of a musical family group that had been giving concerts across the country, he had been singing the same songs, giving the same message, providing the same pat answers wherever he went.

"I've been telling other people they can have answers, but do I have answers myself?" Gaub began to ask himself. "What business do I have preaching to people? Maybe I should quit this itinerant ministry, settle down, and take a permanent job. We travel around so much, I don't know if even God knows where we are."

So Ken Gaub prayed that God would give him an answer. He relates the surprising answer in his book *God's Got Your Number.*

One day Gaub's group stopped in a town in Ohio en route to another concert. While his wife and others in the group went out for lunch, he stayed on the bus to be alone—to think and to pray.

Then he decided to get a Pepsi at a gas station down the street. As he walked there, he heard a phone ring. Alongside the gas station was a phone booth, and the phone continued ringing as Gaub approached. Because it kept on ringing, Gaub went into the booth, picked up the phone, and said, "Hello?"

He heard an operator say, "Person-to-person call for Ken Gaub." He couldn't believe it. He blurted out, "You're crazy! That's impossible." His next thought was that it was a *Candid*

THE REASONS WHY

Not till the loom is
    silent,
And the shuttles
    cease to fly,
Shall God unfold
    the canvas,
And reveal the rea-
    sons why
The dark threads
    are as needful
In the Weaver's
    skillful hand
As the threads of
    gold and silver
In the pattern He
    has planned.
Author Unknown

Camera gag. He looked around to check. Nothing nearby made him think it was a setup.

Then on the phone, he heard someone say, "I believe that's him. I believe that's him." The operator asked again, "Well, is Ken Gaub there?"

Still dubious, Gaub responded slowly, "Yes, I'm Ken Gaub."

In a moment he was talking to a woman who had just written a suicide note and whose life seemed hopeless. She explained that she had just been praying, begging God to show her a way out if he didn't want her to commit suicide. Then she remembered seeing a Christian TV program. Someone named Ken Gaub had been speaking, and he seemed to have been speaking directly to her. If she could only contact him, maybe he would have some answers for her. In her mind she saw a string of numbers and quickly wrote them down. She thought that maybe she was calling the West Coast office of Gaub's group, and so she called person-to-person to make sure she would talk to Gaub himself. Instead, she was connected to a pay phone at an Ohio gas station.

It didn't take much effort for Gaub to convince the woman that God had worked a miracle on her behalf, and soon he talked the woman out of her suicide plan. For the next several months, Ken and his wife stayed in contact with the woman, counseling her regularly until he knew that her suicidal thoughts were behind her.

Gaub is still amazed at the miracle. What are the odds, he wonders, that somebody would think up the number of a phone booth that he happened to be walking by? Could that be a co-incidence? Or was it an amazing answer to the prayers of both Ken Gaub and a distraught woman in a distant state?

Les Lemke's Hidden Talent

You may have seen it as a made-for-TV movie or read about it in *Reader's Digest,* but it's still a story worth retelling.

Abandoned by his parents at Milwaukee Hospital, little Leslie was severely retarded because of cerebral palsy, and because of the disease his eyes had to be removed. He was hopeless, helpless, and totally unwanted.

But May and Joe Lemke decided to take little Leslie into their family anyway. May thought of it as "a job to do for Jesus." And so she gave little Leslie love and care, though at first he couldn't eat, move, or even suck on a bottle. She taught him how to do those basic things and prayed for him every day. Some people thought she was a bit strange to pray for such a hopeless case, but for May, Leslie wasn't a case—he was a person to be loved and prayed for.

He couldn't stand or move at all on his own, but May spent three years patiently showing him how he could get on his feet and even walk a little by holding on to a fence.

Then when Leslie turned twelve years old, a change came. Now May Lemke began praying differently: "Dear Lord, the Bible says that you gave each of us a talent. Please help me find the talent in this boy. He lies there most of the time doing nothing, but if you have given him a talent, help me find it."

Convinced that the Lord would answer her prayer, May and Joe put a piano in Leslie's room and played a variety of music on the radio for him. The piano, of course, remained unused. As for the radio, they couldn't tell if he was paying any attention to the music from it or not.

One night when Leslie was eighteen, May prayed with him as usual and put him to bed. Her prayer was the usual prayer, but she felt more intensity, more earnestness as she prayed. At 3 A.M. she and Joe were awakened by the strains of Tchaikovsky's Piano Concerto no. 1, popularly known as "Tonight We Love." The music was coming from Leslie's room.

Was the TV on? Did the radio somehow get turned on? They went to investigate and found a miracle. Leslie, who had never

He was a Christian and he prayed. He asked for strength to do greater things, but he was given infirmity that he might do better things. He asked for power that he might have the praise of men; he was given weakness that he might feel the need of God.

Anonymous

talked or gotten out of bed by himself, had dragged himself to the piano and was playing and—believe it or not—singing.

May was laughing and crying at the same time. "Oh, thank you, dear Jesus, thank you. You have given the boy a talent. Nobody can ever tell me there is no God and Jesus in this world."

This was no hallucination. In the years since then, Leslie continued to demonstrate his strange talent. He needed to hear a song only once to have it recorded in his mind. Whether the words were in English, French, Italian, or something else—he could repeat it. Experts were baffled. Maybe the part of Leslie's brain that controls musical ability was stimulated in some way, they guessed. It was beyond the ability of science to explain.

Soon the national media picked up the Leslie Lemke story. Network television and *Reader's Digest* featured the story, as did Christian television. For May, it just showed what God can do. "I believed so much in God. . . . I just knew I was going to get something." But what she got from God was a surprise far beyond anything she could imagine.

Miracle Well in the Persian Desert

A hundred thousand gallons a day; that's what Krulak needed. Just one hundred thousand gallons of water a day, every day.

Marine Major General Charles Krulak had the responsibility for supplying the troops, and one hundred thousand gallons was no problem for this experienced officer. Except this was the Gulf War—in the desert.

This was a different kind of war with many new challenges. Leaders of the Allied forces were especially concerned about the possibility of chemical warfare, making the need for water all the more crucial—they'd need it for decontamination. Fortunately for Krulak, the forces were encamped in an area with plenty of wells that could easily pump the huge water quota, if necessary.

But then the troops were ordered seventy-four miles to the northwest, to an area called "the gravel plains." At their new site, Krulak's soldiers desperately dug for water but found only dust. Experts were called in to help, but no matter how hard they searched, they couldn't locate a water source.

For years, General Krulak had made it a practice to meet with his staff officers for morning prayers. In one of those prayer meetings shortly before the ground attack, the critical need for water became the focus of the prayers. But as the staff officers were praying, a colonel interrupted Krulak. "Sir, could you come with me? It's important."

The colonel took him down a road constructed by the Marine Corps and pointed to a pipe rising out of the ground about thirty to fifty yards from the road. A bar on the pipe made it look like a cross. At the base of the pipe were a green diesel generator, a red pump, four new batteries, and a tank containing one thousand gallons of diesel fuel—a fuel not used by U.S. forces.

This was a mystery. Who could have dug this well? Why hadn't it been discovered earlier? Neither General Krulak nor the colonel had any idea. But then Krulak pushed the ignition button, and the generator popped into action, powering the pump, which began drawing water out of the dusty ground. There was a well down there! As it turned out, that well supplied huge amounts of water for the troops—within ten gallons of the one hundred thousand needed per day.

What a miracle! Twenty thousand troops had traveled this road, and not one of them saw this well until Sunday morning as the staff officers prayed for water. "There was no way anyone could have driven down that road and not seen the well and equipment painted in multiple colors," General Krulak told reporters later. "That well was the result of prayers of righteous men and women praying in America . . . and the prayer miracles didn't end with finding the well."

4

Look What You Started

Sometimes a Small Prayer Results in Something Huge

Now to him who is able to do immeasurably more than all we ask or imagine, according to his power that is at work within us, to him be glory throughout all generations, for ever and ever! Amen.

Ephesians 3:20–21

The group leader asked everyone to turn to the appropriate text to begin the Bible study. One visitor piped up, "Shouldn't we begin with prayer?"

"No," the leader replied rather smugly, "I don't believe in using prayer as punctuation."

The truth was, the leader was miffed at the visitor's audacity in suggesting how to run the meeting. Yet he was also resisting the notion that every Bible study meeting had to have a certain format. Nothing is wrong with starting such a meeting in prayer, but do you *have* to?

To be sure, prayer is often used as a kind of punctuation to start meetings of all sorts. Is prayer some sort of magic dust sprinkled on the proceedings? Or a blessing that will make good things automatically follow? Not necessarily.

Nevertheless, Scripture and centuries of Christian experience confirm that great things happen when people start with prayer. It's no magic dust, but a dynamic reliance on the Lord. When we realize how much we need his guidance and power, we know we'd *better* go to him first—because we're nothing without him.

"Unless the LORD builds the house," the psalmist says, "its builders labor in vain" (Ps. 127:1). Savvy construction workers want to get him in on the ground floor.

> *O Son of God, I humbly expect your divine enabling. Hour by hour, in toil, in leisure, in privacy, in company, in success, in adversity, in things sacred, in things secular, in great things, and in least, fill my void with your fulness. May this day be one of divine victory, of peace, of love, of truth, and of power by your Spirit.*
>
> H. C. G. Moule (adapted)

They Weren't Known for Their Praying

No, they hadn't been known for their praying. In fact, seven weeks earlier, Peter, James, and John had fallen asleep when they were supposed to be praying with Jesus. He had asked them, "Couldn't you just pray with me for one hour?" They couldn't. That was probably late in March A.D. 30. Now it was mid-May.

A lot had happened in those seven weeks. Jesus of Nazareth had been crucified and laid in a garden tomb; then on the third day, he had risen from the dead. His disciples could hardly believe it, but there he was, alive again. Jesus had appeared to

47

> "What I tell you in the dark, speak in the daylight; what is whispered in your ear, proclaim from the roofs."
>
> Matthew 10:27

them and other followers numerous times in those weeks. He had even eaten fish with them on the shores of their beloved Galilee. Then one day, with his disciples watching, Jesus ascended into the skies and disappeared from sight. They kept staring into the heavens, but two angels came and announced that Jesus would be coming back someday.

They were stunned. For a moment they must have wondered, "What do we do now?" Soon they remembered his final words: Return to Jerusalem and wait for the promise of the Father. He also said something about being baptized with the Holy Spirit—whatever that meant—and then becoming witnesses to all the world.

Yes, it was staggering, beyond their comprehension. These Galileans had hardly been out of the country. But they walked back to Jerusalem, gathering together in the upper room, where they had met six weeks earlier for the Last Supper. At this point, the group of Jesus followers included eleven of the original twelve disciples (not Judas) and a number of women, including Jesus' mother, Mary. Jesus' brothers, who had earlier doubted Jesus, apparently became believers after the resurrection. About 120 followers of Jesus were now meeting together.

What were they doing? Maybe talking, maybe reviewing the teachings of Jesus, but certainly praying. Those were the last instructions of the Master: Wait and pray until the Holy Spirit arrives. For an active man like Peter, waiting and praying wasn't easy, but he wasn't going to fail this time.

Then ten days after Jesus' ascension, it happened. The Jews called the day Pentecost (meaning "fifty"), because it came on the fiftieth day after Passover. Just as the Feast of Passover brought thousands to the streets of Jerusalem, so did the Feast of Pentecost.

What a day it was! The disciples must have burst from the upper room like football players from the locker room. Was that a tornado sweeping through the temple courts where the crowds had gathered? A "whoosh" of wind, unlike anything the people had ever heard, and then came the 120 disciples—men and women together—praising God in loud voices. At first the temple worshipers couldn't understand them. Local residents could usually discern Galileans by their accent, but this wasn't an accent they were detecting. Foreign visitors were comprehending everything that was said. People from Mesopotamia, from Rome, from northern Turkey, from southern Egypt, from Libya in North Africa—they were all nodding in perfect understanding.

Then Peter got the crowd's attention. The last time he was in the temple courtyard was probably when he denied knowing Jesus. Now he was preaching, quoting passages from Joel and from the Psalms. Obviously, something was different about him now.

But it wasn't just Peter who had changed. In March practically all these disciples had forsaken Jesus and fled in fear. Why were they so different in May? Why were they now acting as if they weren't afraid of anything? Why were they acting as if they could conquer the world?

For ten days they had been praying together, praying for the coming of the Holy Spirit, even though they weren't sure what that meant. They were praying for power, even though they weren't sure where that would take them.

The fisherman's fearless message netted a huge response. About three thousand committed themselves to Jesus, and suddenly there were twenty-five times as many followers of Christ as the day before.

Those upper-room disciples didn't know what to expect when they prayed. They had no idea that some of those who heard would take the gospel back to Rome and Egypt and Mesopotamia and other places they had never heard of. But when the Holy Spirit comes, big things happen.

Two Women of the New Hebrides

A blind woman had a vision. That's how this whole adventure started. Eighty-four-year-old Peggy Smith had lost her eyesight,

> "Call to me and I will answer you and tell you great and unsearchable things you do not know."
>
> Jeremiah 33:3

which prevented her from attending church. But she and her sister Christine, who suffered with severe arthritis, prayed regularly for revival. One day as she prayed, Peggy envisioned the churches in the area packed with young people.

The problem was, most of those churches hadn't seen any young people lately. It was the late 1940s, and in that region—the New Hebrides islands off the coast of Scotland— church attendance was in serious decline. The old faithful still showed up, health permitting, but the new generation stayed away. So Peggy's vision could have been dismissed as wishful thinking. However, she sent for her minister anyway.

As Elmer Towns and Douglas Porter relate the amazing story in their book *The Ten Greatest Revivals Ever,* the minister accepted the vision of crowded churches as a message from God. Pastor James Murray MacKay was familiar with the way these two sisters had turned their humble cottage into a sanctuary for prayer. As it happened, his own wife had experienced a similar dream only a few weeks earlier. He called his church leaders to prayer. For three months, they prayed two nights each week among bales of straw in a local barn, asking God to send revival.

MacKay knew he needed help. He considered inviting Duncan Campbell, an experienced Scottish revivalist, to preach in his parish. But before he could act on it, he received word that Peggy Smith wanted to see him again. God had told her in prayer, she informed him, that Duncan Campbell should be invited to preach. "God is sending revival to our parish," she insisted, "and Mr. Campbell will be his instrument."

It made sense. Campbell had been raised in the highlands of Scotland and spoke fluent Gaelic. MacKay invited the evangelist for ten days of meetings. However, Campbell had other commitments, and so he declined. He said he'd come a year later if they still wanted him.

MacKay broke the news to Peggy.

"That's what the man says," the blind woman replied. "God has said otherwise. Write him again."

50

Unaware of what was going on in the parish of Barvis, Campbell began to wonder whether he had done the right thing in turning down the invitation. A short time later, as he sat in the front row of the famed Keswick Bible Conference, he felt uneasy. He had long dreamed of preaching at Keswick; it was the opportunity of a lifetime. Now, at last, his lifetime dream had been realized.

But as he sat there, he felt strongly that the Holy Spirit wanted him to go immediately to the New Hebrides islands. Turning to the moderator, he excused himself, saying, "Something has come up; I must leave immediately." He caught the next boat to the New Hebrides. When he began preaching in the parish church, the response was immediate. The building was filled beyond capacity. A witness later spoke of "the awful presence of God. . . . Cries for mercy were mingled with shouts of joy."

The revival spread quickly to neighboring districts, "traveling faster than the speed of gossip." A neighboring church asked Campbell to speak at 1:00 A.M., yes, an hour after midnight. He arrived to find a full church with crowds of people outside. The entire New Hebrides was shaken by spiritual revival—even the young people.

Meanwhile, at home, Peggy and Christine Smith explained, "We had a confidence in God that refused to accept defeat." So they kept on praying until the revival came, struggling "through the hours of the night, refusing to quit praying." And God answered.

The Man Who Revived New York City

Hardly anyone remembers his name anymore, and it's little wonder. Jeremiah Lanphier was just a typical New York City businessman. A contemporary described him as "tall, with a pleasant face, an affectionate manner, and indomitable energy and perseverance." Converted when he was thirty-three, in

> If prayer is meager, it is because we consider it supplemental, not fundamental.
>
> J. Oswald Sanders

Charles Finney's Broadway Tabernacle, at age forty-eight he felt called to be an urban missionary.

The North Dutch Reformed Church on Fulton Street in the older downtown section of Manhattan had been losing members. Immigrants were now living in the downtown area, and some other churches had moved uptown. But this church hired Lanphier to call on everyone within walking distance and hand out pamphlets and Bibles. Lanphier wasn't seminary trained and wasn't even a member of the church, but he was eager to do something for the Lord. So he quit his business and started knocking on doors.

Few responded. Lanphier began to wonder if he had made the right decision. He had prayed about it, but now he began to have doubts.

In fact, as a man of prayer, he wondered if other businessmen in New York City valued prayer as much as he did. In his journal he wrote, "One day as I was walking along the streets, the idea was suggested to my mind that an hour of prayer, from twelve to one o'clock, would be beneficial to businessmen." Gradually he developed the idea. It would be held once a week. If a man could drop in for only five or ten minutes, fine. And it would be open to all, not only Wall Street businessmen, but workmen of all trades.

So Lanphier printed up handbills and passed them out. Then at that first noon hour, September 23, 1857, he waited for the men to come. None came; at least no one came during the first half hour. Then one man came, and then another. By one o'clock there were six. The next week there were twenty, the week after that, forty, and then men asked if they could begin meeting every day. By the fourth Wednesday, more than a hundred men were coming. Soon all three of the church's meeting rooms were full, and John Street Methodist Church around the corner was opened to handle the overflow.

Of course, when he printed his handbills for the September 23 opening, Lanphier had no idea that two days later the Bank of Pennsylvania would fail in Philadelphia, sending economic shock waves reverberating across the country. Soon the New York Stock Market crashed. Those who had been trusting in money were suddenly searching for a more reliable master. So the men's prayer meeting was thronged, and new noon prayer meetings began throughout the city. When churches proved to be too small, theaters were hired for the prayer meetings. At Burton's Theater on Chambers Street, crowds came a half hour early, packing the auditorium to capacity, with others waiting outside. On March 19, 1858, the *New York Times* reported that the noted preacher Henry Ward Beecher led three thousand people in prayer at the theater. The *Tribune* and the *Herald* competed with each other for the best coverage of the Manhattan noonday prayer meetings. In April, editor Horace Greeley devoted one entire issue of the *Tribune* to the revival.

Lanphier's Fulton Street prayer meeting became internationally known. Prayer requests came from Switzerland, Germany, and the British Isles.

Converts poured into the churches. In May, one magazine estimated that there were fifty thousand new converts in New York City alone. In cities and towns across the country, prayer meetings began to spring up. A Chicago paper reported, "Nothing like [this] has ever happened in the history of Chicago." Estimates vary regarding the total number of converts. Some say five hundred thousand; others a million.

Jeremiah Lanphier's name isn't as well-known as Dwight Moody's or Billy Graham's, but from the little noonday prayer meeting he started came a conflagration that spread throughout the nation.

Ola Culpepper and Her Optic Neuritis

The year was 1927. Communist political activity was stirring up serious unrest in Shantung, a large province in northeast China. American missionaries were strongly advised by the U.S. government to leave Shantung (now spelled Shandong) and quarter in the Chinese seaport city of Chefoo until things settled down. So Bertha Smith and Ola Culpepper, Baptist missionaries from the United States, made their way to the coast. Lewis and Betty Drummond give the details in their book *Women of Awakenings*.

The Chefoo accommodations left much to be desired. The mission compound there had only two buildings, but more than twenty missionaries gathered there. The political unrest in Shantung was nearly matched by the unrest of these idle missionaries in their cramped quarters. What were they to do? They finally decided to have a spiritual retreat and asked Marie Monsen, a Norwegian Lutheran missionary, to come and share her testimony with them.

"You must confess and forsake all your known sins if God is to fill you with his power," Monsen declared. "God demands holiness." She presented the truths of the Bible regarding godliness, which began a deep soul-stirring and a quest for a true touch from God.

Ola Culpepper, who suffered from optic neuritis, felt the power of the Holy Spirit and became convinced that God wanted to heal her. She had only partial vision in one eye and was in much pain. A world-renowned specialist had examined her, but even he could offer very little hope.

So Ola asked the group of missionaries to pray for her healing. Ask for a miracle? Baptist missionaries didn't do that sort of thing. Oh, they believed in God's power, but they felt he was more likely to provide strength to bear up under misfortune. To ask God to remove the misfortune, well, that was quite unheard of. Ola was obstinate, so she placed her glasses on the mantle of the fireplace, and about twelve missionaries formed a circle around her. Her husband read some verses from the Bible and anointed her head with oil, and all the missionaries placed their hands on her head.

Bertha Smith placed her hand on Ola's head too, but as she reported later, "When I stretched my hand out, I had to bring it back. There facing me was Miss Hartwell, a missionary with whom I had had a little trouble." How could she join in prayer when she harbored a grudge in her heart? So, "right there before everyone," Bertha confessed her bad attitude toward Miss Hartwell. Then they all prayed for Ola.

When they finished praying, two Chinese cooks who had hated each other walked in and interrupted the meeting. After hearing Bertha Smith confessing her sin, they had gone to each other seeking forgiveness and then came to the missionaries saying that they wanted to accept Christ as their Savior.

"For where two or three come together in my name, there am I with them."

Matthew 18:20

Ola Culpepper's husband recalled, "In the midst of our joy for the cooks' salvation, we had completely forgotten Ola's eyes. Then someone remembered and asked, "What about your eyes?"

"They feel all right," she replied, "and the pain is gone." The pain never returned, and Ola left her glasses on the mantle the rest of her life.

But then it was Bertha's turn to speak again, "What kind of missionaries are we?" she asked. She reminded them that they had been confessing their sins to each other and had been praying for Ola's physical eyesight, but had never spent much time praying about the spiritual eyesight of the Chinese to whom they had come as missionaries.

So began the Shantung revival! When the missionaries were allowed to return to Shantung province, they started prayer groups among Chinese leaders and others. Then prayer groups began multiplying everywhere, and the awakening spread and deepened. Though the emphasis was on prayer, not on evangelism, thousands found Christ as Savior as the movement engulfed the land. It was the largest revival any mission in China had ever experienced up to that time.

It all started when a missionary dared to ask others to pray about her optic neuritis.

From Soles to Souls

Dwight L. Moody, who became the most famous evangelist of the nineteenth century, was still a teenager when he saw Chicago for the first time. He had just become a Christian a year earlier

People will be deeply concerned over the issue of prayer in the public schools but will seldom utilize the opportunity to pray for schoolchildren, against which there can be no law.

Richard J. Foster

and had left Massachusetts for Chicago in order to make money. As an aggressive shoe salesman in the Midwest, it didn't take long before he was quite successful.

He also was doing quite well in gathering youngsters into a little mission Sunday school, which didn't stay small very long after Moody got involved. Moody was a veritable Pied Piper, bringing rude and crude youngsters in his tow. However, he showed no sign of becoming the nineteenth century's greatest evangelist. He could bring people to Sunday school, but he wasn't ushering them into the kingdom of God.

Moody tells it this way: "I never spoke . . . about their souls; that was the work of elders, I thought. . . . I thought numbers were everything, so I worked for numbers. . . . Then God opened my eyes."

The turning point came as Moody was pressed into service as a substitute Sunday school teacher. "There was a class of young ladies in the school who were without exception the most frivolous set of girls I ever met. One Sunday the teacher was ill, and I took that class. They laughed in my face, and I felt like opening the door and telling them all to get out and never come back."

Later that week, when Moody talked with the teacher about the horrible situation, he discovered that the teacher had an incurable illness. The teacher explained that he wasn't afraid to die, but he was concerned about his Sunday school class. "I have never led any of my class to Christ," he said. He wanted to do that before he died.

That week Moody accompanied the sick teacher to the home of one of the girls. While there, the teacher asked Moody to pray for the girl's salvation. Moody recalled, "I had never done such a thing in my life as to pray [for] God to convert a young lady there and then. But we prayed, and God answered our prayer."

Then he and the teacher went and talked to the other girls in the class. After prayer, each of the girls surrendered her life to God. In ten days, all of the girls had been converted. And then Moody called the class together with the teacher for a final prayer meeting. The teacher would be leaving the next day, and both Moody and the class of girls knew that death for the teacher was imminent.

They tried to sing a song together and then knelt to pray. Moody said, "I was just rising from my knees when one of the class began to pray for her dying teacher. Another prayed, and another, and before we rose the whole class had prayed!"

Not long afterward, the teacher passed away. No miracle of healing would come for him. Yet one miracle had already happened—the fact that these girls were praying at all—and another miracle was just beginning in the life of Dwight L. Moody.

Later Moody said that the prayer meeting with that class was a pivotal point for him. "There God kindled a fire in my soul that has never gone out. The height of my ambition had been to be a successful merchant, and if I had known that meeting was going to take that ambition out of me, I might not have gone. But how many times I have thanked God since for that meeting!"

This man became the greatest soul winner of his century. Hundreds of thousands, perhaps millions, became Christians through his ministry. He personally talked with nearly 750,000 people about their salvation. All of this began when he prayed one halting prayer for the salvation of an unruly teenage girl in a Chicago tenement.

The C in YMCA

As a teenager, George Williams was just a draper's assistant in a little town named Bridgwater in England's West Country. At age twenty, when he moved to London to better himself, he became just one of 140 draper's assistants in a larger drapery firm at Ludgate Hill.

> The function of the prayer of faith is to turn God's promises into facts of experience.
>
> J. Oswald Sanders

However, something was different about Williams. "The core of his life was prayer," writes biographer John Pollack. A country boy moving to nineteenth-century London had plenty to pray about. Yet more and more Williams found he was praying not for himself but for his 139 fellow workers. In his diary, he would write their names, and then he would plead with God for their salvation.

When he joined the firm, only one other draper was a Christian. But within two years—mostly because of his praying and personal contact—there were twenty. Within three years, regular meetings for prayer had been started, and even the head of the firm attended. The young man from Bridgwater was making an impact.

Though Williams wanted to become a foreign missionary, his friends talked him out of it. They said he had a great mission field within the drapery shops of London, which gave him something else to pray about.

One other draper's assistant joined him in praying for other London shops. Then he gathered twelve young men together in his bedroom to form a society. They sent a letter to every drapery business in the city, then rented a room in a coffeehouse for their meetings, and when they crowded it out, they got a banquet room in a hotel. Some 150 young men came to that first meeting, and George Williams called the new society the Young Men's Christian Association.

The movement was rooted in prayer. Williams writes, "In answer to prayer, we had conversion after conversion." The movement was not aggressively evangelistic, but the decisions for Christ came through prayer and friendship. One by one, YMCAs were begun in other cities and then in other countries. Loosely organized, they were bound together by their common goal: "To unite young men who, regarding Jesus Christ as their God and Saviour according to the Holy Scriptures, desire to be His disciples . . . for the extension of His Kingdom among men."

Williams never quit his work in the business world and eventually became quite successful, but his heart was always with the YMCA, an organization that began because he prayed for his fellow workers. In 1894 the organization celebrated its golden jubilee, and Queen Victoria bestowed upon George Williams the honor of knighthood.

After his death in 1905, the spiritual goals of the YMCA became secondary, but while Sir George was alive, it never drifted from its original goal, the dream that God had given him while he was praying for his fellow draper's assistants.

"Something Too Big for Us"

Grady Wilson was having second thoughts. He was the new guy on the team, and the team was finally visiting the big city—Los Angeles, California. Wilson worried that they were tackling "something too big for us."

The year was 1949, and the team was Billy Graham's evangelistic ministry. Graham's name was not well-known outside of the Midwest and parts of the South, but the Christian Businessmen's Committee of Los Angeles had invited Graham to preach at their annual three-week evangelistic campaign and had put up a huge tent (capacity: six thousand) in an empty downtown lot. The group had also publicized the meetings well. But Grady Wilson, who had just joined the ministry as an associate evangelist, had his doubts. "We still weren't sure," he wrote later. "Perhaps our faith wasn't geared up to it."

One thing, however, made these meetings different. In Los Angeles organized prayer meetings had begun weeks in advance of the crusade; more than a thousand prayer groups were praying regularly. Prayer chains operated around the clock. It was the first time that evangelist Graham had this much prayer power behind him.

For the first two weeks, the meetings seemed pretty ordinary—good crowds, but not up to capacity. As the scheduled closing date drew near, some local supporters asked Graham to extend the meetings another week. Graham wasn't convinced. He had never extended a campaign.

However, because so many people in Los Angeles had been praying for the meetings, Graham considered it. He and associate Cliff Barrows asked the Lord to show them in an unmistakable way whether they should continue in L.A. longer than planned.

After one of the final services, a late-night phone call came from Stuart Hamblen, Southern California's best-known radio personality. He had interviewed Graham on his talk show and had even attended some of the meetings. The preaching had been getting to him, convicting him of his errant ways, so he had decided to leave town. When he returned to hear Graham once again, he became so angry that he stormed out in the middle of the message. On his way home, he stopped in bar after bar. Finally, at 2 A.M. he phoned Graham. The evangelist invited him to come to his hotel. Several hours later, Hamblen accepted Christ. On his radio show that day, he announced, "Tonight at the end of Billy's invitation, I'm going to hit the sawdust trail." The announcement sent shock waves all over California.

That evening the big tent was packed, and also overflowing with reporters and photographers. Flashbulbs popped everywhere. Graham had to ask a photographer to come down from a ladder directly in front of the platform. The next morning, the *Los Angeles Herald Express* and the *Examiner* had banner headlines about the crusade. The aging publisher William Randolph Hearst had sent a two-word telegram to the editors of the Hearst newspapers: "Puff Graham."

No doubt, the crusade now had to be extended. The prayer of Billy Graham and Cliff Barrows had received an answer in the form of banner headlines. They had asked for something unmistakable, hadn't they? The crusade became the talk of L.A. Every evening, thousands arrived early to get seats. The tent was enlarged to accommodate nine thousand.

Other well-known personalities came to Christ. Whenever that happened, the headlines screamed it. Louis Zamperini, Olympic miler and one of America's foremost war heroes, had turned to drink after the war. After hearing Graham, he became

60

a Christian. Most startling was the conversion of twice-convicted felon Jim Vaus, wiretapper and crony of the notorious racketeer Mickey Cohen.

On Sunday, November 20, the campaign's closing day, crowds stood far outside the jammed tent. More than four thousand conversions had been recorded, and magazines like *Life, Time,* and *Newsweek* covered "the rising young evangelist." Graham recalled later, "We had gone to Los Angeles unheralded. When we left we knew that the Spirit of God had moved on that California city as never before."

Some said Graham's success was because William Randolph Hearst had sent out the bulletin, "Puff Graham." But others who knew how God works behind the scenes credited the prayer groups—more than a thousand of them—that had been praying since before the crusade began.

> Thou art coming to
> a King,
> Large petitions
> with thee bring;
> For His grace and
> pow'r are such,
> None can ever ask
> too much!
>
> Anonymous

Bibles and Wild Turkeys

The small town of Boscobel, Wisconsin, advertises itself as the Wild Turkey Hunting Capital of the World and as the birthplace of the Gideons.

Its setting by the Wisconsin River is perfect for wild turkey hunting, but it seems a strange place to give birth to the ministry that puts Bibles in nearly every hotel room on the planet. How it all happened is even more amazing.

September 14, 1898, at 9 P.M., salesman John Nicholson walked into Boscobel's Central Hotel, which of course was the only hotel in town, and requested a quiet room where he could write up his orders. The desk clerk informed him that every room was taken, which in itself was surprising in that small town. But, to be helpful, the clerk suggested that he share room 19 with a stranger, Samuel Hill.

> "With man this is impossible, but with God all things are possible."
>
> Matthew 19:26

Nicholson had no other options, so he agreed. Before crawling into bed that night, Nicholson opened his Bible. At age twelve, he had promised his dying mother he would read the Bible every night at bedtime, and he was keeping that promise as a traveling salesman. His roommate saw what he was doing and said, "Read it aloud. I'm a Christian too."

Nicholson read John 15, and then the two knelt for prayer. That time of prayer began something bigger than they could possibly have imagined. They stayed up until early in the morning, discussing the unique spiritual problems facing Christians who are traveling salesmen.

The two men bumped into each other again on May 31 in Beaver Dam, Wisconsin. Now they decided that maybe God had a purpose in their meetings. Soon they announced plans for an association of Christian salesmen. They set up the first meeting for July 1, 1899, in Janesville, Wisconsin. That town was bigger than Boscobel and not far from Madison, the capital, so maybe they could attract a few more Christian salesmen at such a location. But only three showed up—Nicholson, Hill, and a newcomer, Will J. Knights.

The three men launched their organization to mobilize Christian commercial travelers for encouragement, evangelism, and service. They groped for a name and decided to pray about it. Immediately after they got up from their knees, Knights spoke up, "We shall be called Gideons." The name made a lot of sense. In the Old Testament, Gideon was a layman who was told by God that numbers weren't important. Though he had only three hundred men and was greatly outnumbered, he routed the enemy because God was on his side.

At first, the Gideons' goal was to put a Bible on the reception desk of every hotel, but by 1907 they enlarged their goal to a Bible in every hotel room in the country. Although the Gideons are still best known for their hotel Bibles, they now place Bibles in hospitals, schools, military installations, and prisons.

From the trio of Nicholson, Hill, and Knights, the Gideons now have 140,000 members in 175 countries, distributing

Bibles in eighty languages. About fifty-six million copies of Scripture—or about a million per week—are distributed each year.

What an impressive result of the "chance" meeting and mutual prayer of two strangers in the Wild Turkey Hunting Capital of the World.

What They Found in a Haystack

You might say they were searching for a needle in a haystack. The needle would be a symbolic compass needle—which direction would God lead them? The haystack was real, with real hay.

On August 2, 1806, the weather in western Massachusetts was hot and humid. So Samuel Mills led five of his fellow Williams College students out to Sloane's Meadow, a maple grove near the Hoosac River. Mills called them there to pray. He was a quiet fellow, modest and almost retiring, but a leader nonetheless. He had hardly said, "Let's pray," when a thunderstorm broke out.

Looking for shelter, the students spotted a haystack in a crude shelter and dashed to get under the eaves of the shelter. Sprawling on the hay, they started talking about one of their classes at college, a required geography class. The class had been studying Asia, a continent that was virtually ignorant about Christianity.

Lightning was flashing, thunder crackling, as the students talked excitedly about sending the gospel to Asians who had never heard it, and to the many on that continent who were following Islam. It became a pep rally, with Mills telling the others they could do it if they really wanted to. They knew they would face opposition, but they also knew the power of God. "Come," said Mills, "let's make it the subject of prayer, under the haystack." They all prayed, and as the lightning continued to flash through the sky, Mills closed, praying that "God would strike down with the red artillery of heaven the arm that should be raised against the cross."

Two years later the haystack meeting group developed into a secret society called "the Brethren." Its object was to establish "a mission to the heathen," and every member was "to hold himself in readiness to go on a mission when and where duty may call."

But they had a problem. No money. So they went to the General Association of Massachusetts, composed of Congregational ministers, asking for "advice, direction, and prayers." As a result the American Board of Commissioners for Foreign Missions was founded in 1810. "The Brethren" now numbered six, and all six pledged themselves as America's first foreign missionaries. But that was too many for the board to accept.

It was decided that two of them would not go with the others. If Samuel Mills stayed in the United States, he could recruit future candidates for missionary service. That worked out well, as Mills sent a stream of young men applying for foreign missionary service. But Mills did more. He helped organize the School for Educating Colored Men and later started an African school in New Jersey. He also helped organize the American Bible Society and later worked to resettle some freed slaves in Africa, an effort that led to the formation of the Republic of Liberia.

Adoniram Judson, pioneer missionary to Burma, is often considered the first American foreign missionary, but he was just one of the first four to go in 1812.

By the end of the twentieth century, seventy-one thousand men and women from the United States were serving as overseas missionaries, working in 177 countries, supported by nearly two billion dollars and hundreds of thousands of praying Christians.

You never know what you'll find when you start seeking God's direction in haystacks.

5

Long Distance, Please

God Is Not Bound by Geography

The LORD is near to all who call on him,
to all who call on him in truth.

Psalm 145:18

The world has shrunk. Nowadays you can view an event half a world away as it happens, thanks to satellite broadcasting. You can send instant messages via e-mail to friends on other continents. You can fax documents from your laptop computer to all seven continents at once.

But all this is nothing new to Christians, who have always had a way to stay connected across the miles. We believe God is omnipresent—everywhere at once—and that he hears our prayers. We also believe that his Spirit prompts us, telling us what we should pray for. All of that creates a network that far surpasses any information superhighway. We can pray for anyone in the universe and trust God to hear us.

Sometimes how he answers is pretty remarkable.

Lord of love, you are not far from any of your children.
Watch with your care those who are far away from us. Be
about their path, be within their hearts, be their defense upon
their right hand.

Boyd Carpenter (adapted)

Kidnapping in the Ivory Coast

Did it just happen that thousands of Southern Baptists in America were praying for Travis and Kim Forsythe on May 8, 2000? Or did God have something special in mind?

As many mission agencies and denominations do, Southern Baptists distribute annual prayer calendars, requesting prayer for a different missionary each day of the year. Whenever they could, the planners picked a special day—a birthday or anniversary—in the lives of their missionaries. So that day, Kim Forsythe's thirtieth birthday, was the designated day to pray for her and her husband, serving as missionaries to the Djimini people in Côte d'Ivoire. All across the country, when Baptists looked at the calendar posted on their nightstands, on their coffee tables, or on their bedroom dressers, they paused to pray for the Forsythes.

Good thing.

On that day, Travis Forsythe was driving home with his two-year-old son, Nathanael, to the town of Dabakala. Because of complications from her pregnancy, Kim had been unable to travel with her husband. So on her birthday, she was staying at home with their five-year-old daughter and awaiting her husband's arrival.

As Travis stopped for food late in the day, two bandits seized the car at gunpoint. He clung to the open door of the car, trying to convince the gunmen to let him get little

Nathanael out. One of the gunmen opened fire and wounded the missionary. Then the bandits sped away with the young child in the backseat.

Though he'd been shot in the chest, Travis Forsythe was able to phone authorities immediately about the abduction; he also phoned Southern Baptist missionary leaders, who immediately e-mailed prayer networks across America to pray for little Nathanael Forsythe. Soon the number of people praying for the boy's safety had multiplied; people of all denominations were now praying.

Then a series of unlikely things took place.

What did the kidnappers care about a little child? Life was cheap; they just wanted the car. So forty-five minutes after the abduction, the gunmen put little Nathanael out of the car and left him alone on a dark road in a small village. He might have gone unnoticed all night, but people were praying for him. As it happened, villagers found him and put him in the care of a midwife. She fed and bathed the child and tucked him in bed. Meanwhile the village leaders contacted the authorities to find the parents. It didn't take long before the toddler was reunited with his father and mother. The reunion took place at about 1:30 A.M.

As for Travis Forsythe, doctors discovered that the bullet had passed through his right side between the ribs without hitting any vital organs. Another miracle?

For Kim it was a birthday she will never forget. And we'd have to guess that none of the Forsythes will ever doubt the power of prayer—even when the people praying are thousands of miles away.

Not in Jerusalem alone,
God hears and answers prayer;
Nor on Samaria's mountain lone,
Dispenses blessings there.
But in the secrecy of thought,
Our silent souls may pray;
Or round the household altar brought
Begin and close the day.

James Montgomery

The Spiritual Power of a Bedridden Girl

In the 1860s, a bedridden girl in London wanted to say something to a man four thousand miles away. The telegraph, the telephone, the transatlantic cable—these technological breakthroughs would soon revolutionize long-distance communication, but young Marianne Adlard had another marvel in mind. She asked God to pass along the message for her.

G. Campbell Morgan tells Marianne's story in *The Practice of Prayer*. Marianne had read of the work of evangelist Dwight L. Moody among the ragged children of Chicago. People's lives were being transformed after they listened to this dynamic preacher. She knew that the people of her church needed to hear such a man too. A written invitation might never reach him, and there was no way to talk to him, so Marianne began to pray, "O Lord, send this man to our church."

In 1870 when Moody took his second trip to England, he wasn't planning to do any preaching. He wanted to meet and to learn from Christian leaders like Charles Haddon Spurgeon and George Müller. However, the pastor of Marianne's church met Moody and prevailed upon him to preach there Sunday morning and evening. Moody did, but his Sunday morning sermon accomplished very little. Wherever he preached, it seemed, he found a great openness of spirit, a free response to God's call. But not that morning.

What a crushing blow for Marianne. She had received what she prayed for, but it didn't work. Still, she kept praying.

Then came Sunday evening; after this service, things were entirely different. When Moody asked if any of those present wanted to give their lives to Christ, hundreds rose to their feet. Moody was so surprised that he told them to sit down and then listen while he repeated his request more clearly. They stood up again. Because he still wasn't sure they understood his American English correctly, he asked those who truly wanted to be converted to step into a small chapel near the sanctuary. People crowded in, and extra chairs had to be brought. It was so crowded that Moody suggested that the pastor have a follow-up meeting the next evening to make sure everyone understood what they were doing.

Moody left the next day for Dublin, following his itinerary, but on Tuesday a message came to him from the pastor of Marianne's church: "Come to London at once and help us." More inquirers had come on Monday night than on Sunday, and the pastor needed Moody's help. Moody returned and held meetings for ten days. During that time, four hundred people professed faith in Christ and were received into the church.

> The God of the infinite is the God of the infinitesimal as well.
>
> Dan Crawford

Moody was stunned. He later said that he "wanted to know what this meant." He began making inquiries, and soon he found Marianne Adlard, a bedridden girl, who had been praying "that God would bring me to that church. He had heard her, and brought me over four thousand miles of land and sea to answer her request."

As news spread of what had happened in London, other cities in England and Scotland asked Moody to come. Later, the noted preacher and writer Andrew Murray said that since Moody's visit "the whole religious tone of Scotland has been lifted up." A tone of revival swept throughout the British Isles.

No one remembers Marianne Adlard anymore, but hundreds in her land were thankful that God answered her long-distance prayer regarding Moody: "O Lord, send this man to our church."

The Sinking of the *Titanic*

The day was April 14, 1912. The White Star liner *Titanic* was making its maiden voyage from Southampton, England, to New York City. Dignitaries were aboard, presidents of major American companies, and such prominent people as Astor, Guggenheim, Widener, and Straus. It was the largest vessel afloat, and it was traveling on the Atlantic's most heavily traveled route.

What could possibly happen to such a ship? Colonel Archibald Gracie wasn't worried. He had just taken a delightful swim in the ship's heated pool. "In no swimming bath had I ever enjoyed such pleasure before," he said.

In New York City, however, Gracie's wife was troubled for some strange reason. She couldn't sleep. It wasn't simply sleeplessness; it was anxiety, a kind of anxiety she hadn't experienced before. What was the problem?

She got out of bed, grabbed her prayer book, then fell to her knees. The book opened to the prayer "For Those at Sea," which she prayed on her husband's behalf. Mrs. Gracie prayed earnestly until 5 A.M. and then seemed to be at peace. She went back to bed, fell asleep, and rested until she was awakened by her sister at 8 A.M.

Her sister had a newspaper in her hands. "Sad news," she said, "tragic news." The headlines made it clear enough. The *Titanic* had sunk.

As for her husband, Colonel Gracie, he had been asleep in his cabin when he was awakened by a sudden shock and noise. He got dressed quickly and went down to the deck, where he learned the ship had collided with an iceberg.

After helping women and children into lifeboats, he sank into the ocean with the ship. As he later wrote:

> I was in a whirlpool, swirling round and round, as I still tried to cling to the railing as the ship plunged to the depths below. Down, down, I went: it seemed a great distance. . . . Ascending back to the surface, I could see no *Titanic*. She had entirely disappeared beneath the surface of the ocean without a sign of any wave. A thin light-gray smoke vapor hung like a pall a few feet above the sea. There arose the most horrible sounds ever heard by mortal man, the agonizing cries of death from over a thousand throats.

For a while Gracie bobbed in the icy waters, but then he remembered reading of sailors being scalded to death when, in a shipwreck, the ship's boilers had exploded beneath them. He swam vigorously to get away from the wreckage. With his strength almost gone and his body slowly freezing, he nearly gave up. He prayed that his wife might be comforted when she heard of his drowning, and he asked the Lord to give her this message: "Good-bye, until we meet again in heaven."

Then, from somewhere, he was suddenly filled with new strength. Pushing himself upward, he collided with some of the ship's wreckage. To his left, he spied an overturned lifeboat. About a dozen men had climbed on its bottom and were clinging to it as best they could. Gracie swam toward the boat. As he got nearer, he grabbed the arm of one of the young men and threw his right leg across the boat, pulling himself aboard.

Some 1,513 people perished that night. Colonel Archibald Gracie was one of the survivors. His wife, praying in New York at exactly the time of her husband's greatest need, had no doubt that God had worked a miracle because she had prayed. Colonel Gracie called it a case "of Providential deliverance directly attributable to prayer."

"Stay in the Net"

When Jim Dozier was just a boy in Sunday school, his mother often said to him, "God created you for a purpose, Jim, and the way to fulfill it is to keep in close touch with him."

When he joined the army, another phrase was drilled into him: "Stay in the net." That is, keep in radio communication with your commander when you are out in the field.

Both of those phrases were more relevant than ever when the Italian Red Brigades captured him in 1981.

Jim Dozier was now General James L. Dozier, deputy chief of staff for logistics with the North Atlantic Treaty Organization. A week before Christmas, his wife was preparing dinner for the two of them in their Verona, Italy, apartment when the doorbell rang. The two men said they were plumbers and wanted to check the apartment to see if anything was leaking. Once inside, they pulled out pistols and identified themselves: "We are the Red Brigades." This group had terrorized Italy, kid-

> We can accustom ourselves to a continual conversation with Him. . . . All we need to do is recognize God is intimately present with us, and address Him every moment.
>
> Brother Lawrence

napping and murdering many of the country's top government and business leaders. Italy's former prime minister had been found dead in a car trunk after he was kidnapped by the Red Brigades.

Dozier couldn't tell what they were doing to his wife. All he knew was that he was being stuffed into a large trunk and then carried downstairs. As he figured it, he was put into the back of a truck; then after a long ride, the trunk was lugged into a building. An elevator took him up, then down, and finally he was put on a metal cot in a small tent, six feet square. Three masked men chained him to the cot, took off his gag and blindfold, and then showed him a chemical toilet in the corner.

How long they would keep him there, he didn't know, but obviously they didn't plan to shoot him immediately.

Dozier prayed for his wife and for his adult son and daughter. As a military man who had gone through dangerous combat experiences, he did not fear death himself. He knew that heaven awaited him. He focused on those two phrases: "Stay in the net" and "Keep in touch with him." He knew that he had lost contact with his military commander, but he was still in touch with the divine commander. He needed that assurance, and that night he went to sleep and slept well.

The next day the Red Brigades began questioning him about NATO and about his own political beliefs, and he answered by supplying harmless information.

He sensed that his wife was praying for him, even as he was praying for her. For some reason, he got a vivid impression of an executive officer, and he realized that this man would also be praying for him at that time. And then he thought of another, a schoolteacher in Verona, and still another, a missionary in Vicenza, both of whom would be praying. He realized that American officials and Italian officials would be trying to free him, but he knew that nothing was more powerful than prayer. If this situation were to have a positive outcome, it would be because of prayer.

Christmas passed without any change in his situation. The guards somehow knew that his son and daughter had arrived in Verona, and they gave him a newsmagazine, where he read a rumor of his own death.

Weeks passed. Jim estimated that it was forty days, and he reminded himself that Jesus had spent forty days in the wilderness. He had a strange feeling that God would rescue him soon. Where did that thought come from?

Suddenly he heard wood splintering outside his tent, then shouting and scuffling. His guard aimed a pistol at him, but then a masked man burst in and knocked the guard unconscious.

A member of a rival gang? Jim wasn't sure at first, but then he learned it was a commando from Italy's antiterrorism unit. Six thousand Italian investigators, working closely with American and European intelligence, had followed up thousands of clues until they came to an apartment building in Padua, forty-eight miles from Verona.

"Stay in the net." "Keep in touch with him." Good advice even if you're not being kidnapped by terrorists.

A Verse for Vietnam

He didn't read it very often, but he carried it with him every day. That Gideon New Testament was safely tucked away in his shirt pocket as Jim Stegalls went about his business. His business was war. In Vietnam.

Stegalls had gone to 'Nam when he was nineteen, and now he had just marked his twenty-first birthday. It didn't get any easier. His buddies were dying around him, and he didn't know how much more of it he could take.

February 26, 1968, was a special day for Jim. This was the day when he prayed fervently for the war to end. He prayed for a cease-fire at least, but the message he received in his heart was that he would be killed before nightfall.

So he was not surprised when the enemy launched a ferocious barrage that day. The rockets were landing all around

I cannot tell why
  there should come
  to me
A thought of some-
  one miles and
  years away
In swift insistence
  on the memory,
Unless there be a
  need that I should
  pray.
We are too busy
  even to spare a
  thought
For days together of
  some friends away;
Perhaps God does it
  for us; and we
  ought
To read His signal
  as a sign to pray.

Marianne
Farningham

him, and then he saw one coming straight at him. This would surely be the end for him.

Just before the rocket hit, a buddy pushed him into a grease pit. The two of them waited for a deafening explosion, but no explosion came. The fuse had malfunctioned. It was a dud.

For the next five hours, Jim stayed in the pit. Then, still shaking, he pulled out his neglected New Testament and began reading at the beginning of Matthew. He read eighteen chapters before he stopped at a verse that said, "For where two or three are gathered together in my name, there am I in the midst of them" (Matt. 18:20 KJV). After reading that verse, "I somehow knew things would be all right," Jim recalled later.

Jim survived the war and came home safely. Five years later, he was visiting in the home of his wife's grandmother, Mrs. Harris, who told him a surprising story.

Several years before, she said, when Jim was in Vietnam, she couldn't sleep one night. It was more than sleeplessness—she was terrified. She felt Jim was in danger and desperately needed prayer, so she began praying for him. She wanted to kneel in prayer, but she couldn't because of her arthritis. Instead she fell to the floor and prayed and read her Bible the rest of the night. Early the next morning, she read in her version of Scripture, "If two of you agree down here on earth concerning anything you ask for, my Father in heaven will do it for you. For where two or three gather together because they are mine, I will be right there among them" (Matt. 18:19–20 TLB). When she saw the words, "If two of you agree," she decided she needed to get someone to join her in prayer.

Early the next morning, she woke up her Sunday school teacher and asked her to come over as soon as she could and pray with her for Jim. The two prayed together, claiming the promise of Matthew 18:19–20.

Jim listened to the story in amazement. But he was even more amazed when Mrs. Harris reached for her Bible and opened it to show how she had marked the passage. Alongside the verses in Matthew 18, she had written: "Jim, February 26, 1968."

6

Just in the Nick of Time

*When God's Answer Comes a Moment before
It Would Have Been Too Late*

Before they call I will answer;
    while they are still speaking I will hear.

Isaiah 65:24

Down by one, ten seconds left, the point guard calmly bounces the basketball as he strolls down the court. What's he doing? Time is running out! But he has a plan.

Five. Four. Three. He dribbles twice, evades a defender, and jumps up to toss a high arc toward the basket.

Two. One. The ball drops through the net as the buzzer sounds. Victory!

Never a doubt, the player smiles. He had that winning shot planned.

We forget sometimes that our God created time, that he lives outside of time, and that he knows just what we need when we need it. We get nervous when he waits until the last possible moment to answer our prayers. Why does he do that? Does he want us to worry?

No, he wants us to trust him. Ever since the Israelites saw bread falling from heaven, human beings have tried to bank God's blessings—and it hasn't worked. We think if we store away some manna, we'll be ready for any rainy day. But that just keeps us from turning to God tomorrow.

God blesses us day to day, moment by moment. His mercies are "new every morning." He provides us with "daily bread." Sometimes it might seem that he's waiting until the last possible moment, but he has a plan for ultimate victory. *Never a doubt!*

> *Hear my prayer, O LORD;*
> *   let my cry for help come to you.*
> *Do not hide your face from me*
> *   when I am in distress.*
> *Turn your ear to me;*
> *   when I call, answer me quickly.*
>
> Psalm 102:1–2

Saved by a Cloud

As the soldiers stepped out of the woods, they were met with a barrage of bullets from three nests of German machine guns. Yet they had to cross that clearing. It looked as if they would have to make a mad dash, losing many lives in the process.

It was March 1945, and the U.S. Army's 35th Infantry Division, 137th Infantry, Company I, was making its way through the dense woods of the German Rhineland. Their orders were to capture the town of Ossenburg. As they pushed carefully through the woods, they got word that the company ahead of them had been badly shot up. Company I was the replacement.

One of the GIs, twenty-four-year-old Spencer January, tells the story. "When my company arrived at the scene, I was appalled by the grimness of the situation. Only a handful of wounded, bleeding soldiers hiding behind a large stone house at the edge of the woods had survived. The route to Ossenburg had been completely barricaded."

The machine guns had them pinned down, and there seemed no way to dislodge those gunners. The nests were impenetrable, protected by a small hill. If the GIs could just cross that clearing, they could reach their objective—but such a move would be very risky. How many of them would take machine-gun fire? Spencer January realized he might never get home again to his wife and five-month-old son. The situation seemed hopeless.

Then the order was given to advance. Spencer prayed in desperation. "God, you've got to do something. Please, God, do something."

As he grabbed his M-1 rifle and started forward, a miracle happened. He could hardly believe it. "I stared in amazement. A cloud—a long, fluffy white cloud—had appeared instantly out of nowhere. It moved in over the trees, obscuring the Germans' line of fire."

The American soldiers dashed for the other side of the clearing, dragging the wounded with them. When they reached the trees, they threw themselves under cover. "I watched," Spencer recalled, "as the last American soldier frantically raced toward us in the woods. I will never forget what happened next. The instant the last soldier scrambled to safety, the cloud vanished! Poof! It was gone." The day was once again bright and sunny. Safe in the woods on the other side of the clearing, Spencer thought, *This has to be God's doing.*

Thinking that they still had the American soldiers pinned down behind the stone house, the Germans radioed its position to their artillery. Moments later, the stone house that had sheltered the American soldiers on the other side of the clearing was blown to bits by German artillery. Meanwhile, the Americans went on to capture the city.

An answer to Spencer January's desperate prayer? Yes, but another person was praying as well.

Two weeks later, Spencer got a letter from his mother in Dallas. "What in the world was the matter on the morning of March 9?" she wrote. "You remember Mrs. Tankersly from our church? Well, she called me that morning and said that the Lord had awakened her at one o'clock in the night and said, 'Spencer is in serious trouble. Get up now and pray for him!'" So Mrs. Tankersly had prayed all night, until six in the morning, when she had to get ready for work. Just before she got up from her knees, she prayed, "Lord, whatever danger Spencer is in, just cover him with a cloud."

When Spencer calculated the time difference, he discovered that Mrs. Tankersly had prayed at exactly the same time that he was approaching that deadly clearing. And 6:00 A.M. in Dallas was the same time that Company I made its dash for safety, covered by a cloud. The Lord had sent the cloud at the request of Mrs. Tankersly, just in the nick of time.

Spencer January wrote, "From that moment on, I intensified my prayer life. . . . I am convinced there is no substitute for the power of prayer."

> FREE
>
> No postage stamps for prayers we send,
> The mails do not affect them;
> They go without a second's pause
> The moment we direct them.
>
> Mildred N. Hoyer

The Miracle at Valley Forge

A Pennsylvania farmer was walking quietly through the woods one day in the winter of 1777–78 when he saw a man on his knees. Could the body be frozen there, a victim of the harsh cold? No, as the farmer drew closer, he heard the man speaking, but not to him. The man was praying, fervently begging the Lord to provide guidance, protection, and food for his men.

Then the farmer recognized the kneeling man. It was George Washington.

While Washington's troops encamped at Valley Forge that cruel winter, the general often prayed in this secluded forest glen. It was a crucial time in the American Revolution, a time to gather troops and train them to fight a better-organized British army. With bitter cold and scant provisions, however, Washington was more concerned about keeping his men alive. No wonder the general turned to the Lord in prayer.

The eavesdropping farmer, Isaac Potts, listened to Washington for a while, awed by his fervency. Then he crept home, telling his wife, "If there is anyone on earth whom the Lord will hearken to, it is George Washington."

The soldiers were a ragtag bunch, drawn from the farms and shops, with no military experience. The winter of 1777–78 would prove to be their testing ground. Valley Forge had seemed a good location for Washington and his men to spend the winter—only fifteen miles from Philadelphia and easy to defend. But Washington wasn't prepared for the ferocious weather. His troops were already painfully short of shoes, clothing, blankets, and tents.

As the winter progressed, the situation only got worse. Food became so scarce that the soldiers went for days without anything to eat. When they did eat, it was likely to be less than a quarter cup of rice and a tablespoon of vinegar. During the months of January and February, more than four thousand soldiers were suffering severely from exposure, disease, and starvation. One in four died of exposure.

During these difficult times, George Washington prayed for God's protection. An officer who was at Valley Forge said of Washington, "On every practicable occasion, he sought God's blessing, and when no chaplain was present, he often called his staff officers around him and lifted his heart and voice in prayer."

Often the general prayed for food for his men. In mid-February, he wrote, "This army must inevitably be reduced to one or the other of these three things: starve, dissolve, or disperse, in order to obtain subsistence."

Some five hundred horses starved to death, and because the ground was frozen, their carcasses rotted about the camp. Historian Christopher Ward says, "The soldiers themselves were not much better off than the horses." In mid-February, Washington wrote, "A part of the army has been a week without any kind of flesh and the rest three or four days."

Washington had appointed Nathanael Greene to forage the countryside for food, "to search the country through and through." But the country, he found, was already "very much drained. . . . The country has been so much gleaned that there is little left in it," Greene reported back to Washington.

Then came one miraculous answer to Washington's prayer for food, as Bruce Lancaster describes in his book *The American Revolution:*

> One foggy morning the soldiers noticed the Schuylkill River seemed to be boiling. The disturbance was caused by thousands and thousands of shad which were making their way upstream in an unusually early migration. With pitchforks and shovels, the men plunged into the water, throwing the fish onto the banks. Lee's dragoons rode their horses into the stream to keep the shad from swimming on out of reach. Suddenly and wonderfully, there was plenty of food for the army.

Another historian chronicles, "It was like manna from heaven. . . . The soldiers ate to repletion, and hundreds of barrels of the fat fish were salted down for future use."

The harvest of fish came just in the nick of time.

Livingstone's Lion

The children wanted their friend to be safe. They had learned enough about Africa to know that life could be dangerous there. So when the members of this Scottish Sunday school class wrote to missionary-explorer David Livingstone, assuring him of their prayers, they enclosed a small financial gift. This money, they said, had a special purpose: Livingstone should use it to hire a personal attendant to look out for him.

Though Livingstone valued his independence, he also recognized the children's concern for him. So he hired an African named Mebalwe to become his personal attendant.

On February 16, 1844, some Africans told Livingstone that lions were in the area. These lions were especially troublesome because they killed livestock even in the daytime. An entire African village was in panic. Livingstone and Mebalwe joined a group of Africans in the hunt.

One lion was sighted on a small hill. The Africans made a semicircle around the lion as Livingstone and Mebalwe cautiously approached. Mebalwe fired first and hit the rock on which the lion was perched. The lion snarled and leaped away, breaking through the circle behind him. Then two more lions were spotted; a new circle was formed, but Livingstone hesitated to shoot because of the possibility of hitting one of the Africans. Some of the posse gave up as Livingstone went to the far side of the hill.

There he saw the lone lion again. Livingstone took aim and fired both barrels. He hit his target, but the lion was only wounded. Pausing to reload his weapon, he heard a shout. He looked around and saw the huge lion leaping toward him. The lion's jaws fixed on Livingstone's left shoulder, crushing the shoulder bone. Then the lion shook Livingstone, as a "terrier dog does a rat," the missionary described later. He was in shock, though he says he was "quite conscious of all that was happening."

As the lion's paw was on the back of his head, Livingstone looked around and saw Mebalwe aiming at the lion from a distance of ten to fifteen yards. When he fired at the beast, the lion left Livingstone to charge at Mebalwe. Finally, the lion's gunshot wounds took effect and the animal dropped dead. The other lions went slinking into the bush.

Livingstone's injuries were both severe and painful, and he lived the rest of his life with a badly wounded shoulder. But thanks to Mebalwe—and thanks to the prayers and the offering of a Sunday school class in Scotland—Livingstone's great explorations in Africa lay ahead of him.

Sometimes God asks us to answer our own prayers. That is, he invites us to participate in the answers he provides. Yes, he works miracles, but sometimes he works through us. Those Scottish children understood all that. Besides praying for Livingstone's safety, they contributed to it. God used their prayers, their money, and an alert attendant to protect this pioneering missionary, just in the nick of time. As a result, Livingstone lived for nearly thirty more years and opened an entire continent to the Christian gospel.

The Rescue of "Hernia City"

In 1987 fifty-five-year-old Dr. Harold Adolph left his comfortable practice as a surgeon in a Chicago suburb. Why? Because he felt that God wanted him to work in an inadequately equipped, understaffed hospital on the south edge of the Sahara Desert.

There at the one-hundred-bed Galmi Hospital in sunbaked, dusty Niger, Adolph would do almost every imaginable kind of surgery. He had previously specialized in certain types of surgery, but now he would operate on all sorts of ailments, from head to toe. He was accustomed to doing one or two surgeries a day, maybe forty in a month. Now he performed as many as forty surgeries a week! Cataract extractions, anterior spinal fusions, hernia repairs, removal of giant tumors, you name it.

When Harold Adolph, a quiet-spoken, gangling six-footer, and his wife, Bonnie Jo, first arrived in south central Niger, they found political unrest and a country wracked by civil war. Not only that, but Galmi Hospital was severely understaffed, and employees were striking for more money. Adolph and his staff of four other doctors and six nurses were treating an average of four hundred patients a day. Many of the patients walked or were carried by relatives—some for days—to get to the hospital, and others arrived by donkey or ox cart, bush taxi, and even camel.

"Surgery on the edge of the desert tends to be dominated by tropical infectious disease, which frequently requires operative therapy," according to Adolph. Typhoid fever, he explains, often causes perforation of the small intestine, requiring surgery. As a result, many patients would come in with strangulated hernias. (One short-term missionary surgeon called Galmi Hospital "Hernia City.") And sometimes fracture surgery was needed to compensate for the botched work of a witch doctor who tried to fix a broken bone with sticks and twine.

Within a few months of Adolph's arrival, the hospital was in danger of closing. Besides its other problems, it needed more money to continue, and there was no foreseeable way to raise enough funds.

Somehow Dr. Adolph remained optimistic that God would keep the hospital open. "We had just moved into our three new operating rooms, and they were inadequately equipped," he recalls. "We needed operating tables to replace ancient ones, oxygen concentrators, anesthesia machines, automatic blood pressure monitors—you name it. We had no funds to purchase this equipment. People were responding to the gospel as never before, and I believed Satan wanted us out of business. God spoke to me through Acts 18:9–10 to be 'courageous, do not give up; I have many people who need to hear the gospel.'"

For years Adolph had observed a custom of praying with patients before their surgery, and that custom became the means of an amazing answer to prayer, just in the nick of time.

Years before he went to Africa, when he was practicing medicine in the United States, he once prayed with a woman about to undergo gall bladder surgery. It seemed like a routine operation for him, but it wasn't to the woman. After her recuperation, the woman, an unmarried schoolteacher and a former nun, brought him baked treats from her oven as her way of saying thanks. Later, miffed by the treatment of certain relatives, she took them out of her will, designating their half of her estate for the ministry of Galmi Hospital in Niger, where her favorite doctor had gone.

As it happened, the woman died in 1996. About the time the Galmi facility was to close its doors forever, her legacy arrived—nearly one hundred thousand dollars—enough to purchase most of the hospital's needed equipment. Dr. Adolph's prayers had been answered in a most surprising way. Galmi Hospital could remain open.

Now retired, Dr. Adolph travels as many as fifty thousand miles a year to ask doctors and medical students to do as he did and commit themselves to overseas service. With a slight smile he adds, "The pay and retirement benefits are out of this world."

Rickenbacker and the Seagull

Eddie Rickenbacker was the ace of America's fighter pilots. Once a professional race-car driver, he became the leading flier for the United States in World War I, shooting down twenty-two German planes and four observation balloons—despite being initially turned down as a pilot because at twenty-six he was considered too old.

After World War I, Rickenbacker owned an automobile company and then bought Eastern Airlines, becoming its president and general manager. When the United States entered World War II after the Pearl Harbor attack, pilots with combat experience were sorely needed, so Rickenbacker was pressed into service, though he was now past fifty. He was quickly given special missions to Iceland, England, and the South Pacific.

In 1942 Rickenbacker was chosen to take an important message to General Douglas MacArthur, headquartered in New Guinea. Flying over the South Pacific, Rickenbacker's crew got lost and strayed out of radio contact. Fuel ran low, and they had to ditch their B-17 in the ocean. Boarding three rafts, the eight-man crew floated in the vast Pacific. At night, sharks rammed their rafts; during the day, the men worked to protect themselves from the hot sun and occasional storms.

Rations ran out after eight days; they felt they would die of thirst. Their chance of rescue seemed remote at best. Only a miracle could save them now.

So they prayed. Captain Cherry, who had a prayer book, led a service every afternoon. But the hot Pacific sun took its toll, and the men felt increasingly lethargic and depressed. Days stretched into weeks.

Later Sergeant Johnny Bartek recalled the harrowing experience:

> As soon as we were in the rafts at the mercy of God, we realized that we were not in any condition to expect help from him. We spent many hours of each day confessing our sins to one another and to God. . . .
>
> Then we prayed—and God answered. It was real. We needed water. We prayed for water and we got water—all we needed. Then we asked for fish, and we got fish.

Then they began to pray for meat. Soon afterward, when William Cherry ended his prayer for deliverance, the men sang a hymn of praise. Rickenbacker joined in, though he was amazed that his men could still praise God for anything. After the hymn, as the men talked with one another, Rickenbacker began to doze, pulling his hat brim over his eyes. *God must do something soon, or we'll all die,* he said to himself. It was half a prayer.

Suddenly he felt something heavy on his head; it seemed to be scratching at him. Was he going mad? *No,* he thought, *a seagull has landed on my head. A seagull? In the middle of the ocean? It can't be.* Seagulls were coastal birds, ill-suited for the high seas. But as Rickenbacker peered out from under his hat, he saw the other men staring at him—or rather at *it.* He knew he would have to grab the gull quickly before it flew off. He readied his hands at his side, flexing his fingers, then quickly reached up, grabbing the bird as forcefully as he could. The gull tried desperately to escape, but Rickenbacker held on. The raft was rocking now; the men nearest him were grabbing for the bird too. A few seconds later, they pinned the screeching bird to the raft. They ate the bird and used the intestines for bait to catch fish.

Bartek was in awe. "Seagulls don't go around sitting on people's heads waiting to be caught!" he wrote.

But it was more than food that buoyed the men's spirits. They knew that God had heard their prayer and answered it. A lone seagull had no reason to be out in the middle of the ocean, unless God had sent it. And after twenty-three days lost in the middle of the Pacific, Eddie Rickenbacker and his crew were rescued, just in the nick of time.

Many amazing stories emerged from World War II, many amazing answers to prayer, but no one has yet explained the seagull that just happened to land on Captain Rickenbacker's head in the middle of the Pacific.

Why the Baker Couldn't Sleep

If you've read *Oliver Twist* or even seen the movie, you have some idea of the plight of orphans in nineteenth-century England. In the grip of poverty, such children were destined for workhouses or lives of crime. Yet a year before Charles Dickens penned that eye-opening classic, a man named George Müller was starting his first home for orphans in Bristol, England. And Müller's work was powered by prayer.

That first year, 1836, Müller's home had thirty children the second year, sixty. The orphanage kept growing, and Müller kept praying that the Lord would send enough money, and the Lord always did. Through prayer and extraordinary faith, telling no one but God of his needs for funds, Müller built orphanage after orphanage until in 1875 he was caring for two thousand children, giving them a happy home and instructing them in Christianity. Sometimes his staff wasn't sure where tomorrow's bread would come from, but Müller reminded them that the Lord's Prayer said nothing about "tomorrow's bread." God supplies our *daily* bread.

Numerous stories are told about the way God answered Müller's prayers in the nick of time.

One day when the daughter of a friend was visiting him, the girl told him, "I wish God would answer my prayers like he does yours."

"He will," Müller responded. Then, taking her on his knee, he quoted the verse, "What things soever ye desire, when ye pray, believe that ye receive them, and ye shall have them" (Mark 11:24 KJV).

One morning he took her by the hand and led her down into the dining hall where the orphans were waiting for food. No food was available. Nothing was on the tables except empty dishes.

In a loud voice, Müller said grace: "Dear Father, we thank thee for what thou art going to give us to eat." Still there was no food.

Then came a knock at the door. It was a baker. "Mr. Müller," the baker said, "I couldn't sleep last night. Somehow I felt you didn't have bread for breakfast, and the Lord wanted me to send you some. So I got up at two o'clock and baked some fresh bread, and have brought it for you."

Müller thanked the baker, took the bread inside to the staff, and then stopped to publicly praise God for his provision. "Not only bread," he noted, "but fresh bread."

Then came a second knock. This time it was a milkman. He announced that his milk cart had broken down outside the orphanage. He wondered if the orphanage could use some fresh cans of milk, because he would have to empty his wagon in order to repair it.

After the little girl saw how prayer after prayer of George Müller's was answered miraculously, she began ending her own prayers in a different way. Instead of asking God to answer her prayers "in Jesus' name," she said, "like you do George Müller's."

7

Out of the Ordinary

Even Commonplace Things Can Be God's Instruments

> "Which of you, if his son asks for bread, will give him a stone? Or if he asks for a fish, will give him a snake? If you, then, though you are evil, know how to give good gifts to your children, how much more will your Father in heaven give good gifts to those who ask him!"
>
> Matthew 7:9–11

Sometimes God's tiny answers are more amazing than his huge ones. If you truly believe in God, it's no stretch to believe in his power. After all, he's the Creator of the universe. He can certainly bend the rules of the natural order if he so chooses. And he's the one who made us, so he can accomplish all sorts of healing and leading in our lives.

It's not a question of what he *can* do, but what he *will* do. Why would he bother with anything as ordinary as our daily bread? Jesus said that the Father knows whenever a sparrow falls. Of course he has the ability to know that, but why would he care? Shouldn't he free up his divine radar screen for more important things?

You're about to read about a number of answers to prayer that seem downright silly. You might wonder how these people dared to bring such trivial requests before the almighty God. Yet remember the disciples who tried to keep children away from Jesus. Like modern celebrity handlers, they wanted to keep Jesus focused on truly important matters. But Jesus rebuked them; children were important to him. So are our simple, childlike requests.

> *Give us hinds' feet that we may climb and stand*
> *In the high places of Thy promised land;*
> *Held ever only by Thy strong right hand.*
>
> *And may we from this Mount of God descend*
> *To meet the duties which each path attend,*
> *Resolved to serve Thee only to the end.*

Anonymous

I Want Three Ripe Tomatoes, John

"I want three ripe tomatoes, John," Mina cried out in her near delirium. Her fever was dangerously high, and she was dying. Her husband, John, wanted to explain that it was impossible to get three ripe tomatoes, but she wasn't listening to reason.

John and Mina Clark were serving as missionaries with the Africa Inland Mission in the very primitive northeastern corner of what was then called the Belgian Congo. It was the first half of the twentieth century, before missionary aviation could bring medical help within hours.

"I want three ripe tomatoes!" Mina was calling again. How could John calm her? In the Congo no one had ever heard of tomatoes. All he could do was fall to his knees and pray. His prayer was

90

long and rambling, not always making sense. He was simply blubbering from the depths of his heart, but God knew what he meant. John asked God to heal Mina, perhaps to send a doctor—though it would take a week for a doctor to get to this jungle outpost. And yes, he also prayed for tomatoes.

> There is nothing too great for God's power, and there is nothing too small for His love.
>
> Rosalind Goforth

The next day, one of the local tribesmen knocked at the Clarks' door. With him was a woman from a neighboring tribe. In her arms she carried a basket covered with a banana leaf. After some casual conversation, the woman explained why she had come. About a month earlier, John Clark had visited her tribe. She figured that he, as a foreigner, might be able to help.

What was her problem?

"Some time ago, a traveler left seed with us," she explained, "and I planted it. The plant has now borne a harvest, but I am afraid to eat them, as I do not know whether or not they are poison."

John Clark lifted the banana leaf and saw something astonishing in her basket—ripe, red tomatoes. Three of them.

The woman saw the missionary's obvious delight. "You can have these," she said, "for I have many, many more at home."

John thanked the woman profusely and then took the three tomatoes to Mina. Shortly thereafter, the doctor arrived, ahead of schedule, and soon Mina was on the road to recovery. John never knew whether the doctor's medicine or the miraculous tomatoes had more to do with her recovery. Whichever, he knew it was God's amazing answer to prayer.

As he thought through these events, John realized something even more amazing. God must have planned all of this long in advance. God must have known when that traveler would give the seed to the African tribeswoman. God must have known when the woman would plant the seeds and when the tomatoes would ripen. And God must have directed the woman to come to his mission station on the day after he had prayed for three ripe tomatoes to appear out of nowhere.

Amazing!

Does God Care about Angel Food Loaf Cakes?

"Crumbling, jagged, malformed jelly rolls." That's all Lynne saw in front of her. And it was driving her into a panic.

The job seemed easy enough: Bake 220 small angel food cake rolls for the church's annual Christmas tea. Lynne Hall was new to the Crossroads Baptist Church in Bellevue, Washington, and she wanted to make a good impression. She had seen a recipe for these cake rolls in a book, and the photograph of the finished product looked great. All you needed were thirty angel food loaf cakes, which you would then cut, spread with jam, and roll up.

So Lynne ordered the cakes at the bakery. When her order arrived, she took them home to transform them into jelly rolls. So far, so good. But the bakery hadn't delivered what it had promised; the cakes were raw in the middle. Lynne got some replacements, but these weren't right either. She certainly couldn't bring these "crumbling, jagged, malformed" pastries to the Christmas tea.

Desperate, she visited all the bakeries in the area, but all gave her the same reply: They didn't have time to give her what she wanted. And the tea was the very next day.

As she drove to the last bakery outlet in the area, tears were streaming down her face. She started praying. Lynne admits she was "pretty new to the idea of prayer," since she had only recently become a Christian. Previously she had thought that people needed to pray only "for big things, and that you wouldn't bother God with the minor details of life." What did God care about jelly rolls? But she knew that God cared about *her*, and so she turned to him in her culinary crisis.

"Dear God," she prayed as she steered into the last bakery, "please may there be angel food loaf cakes here." She understood how trivial it sounded, but she prayed anyway. "And God," she added, "not the tube kind either; I need the loaf kind, God. Please, God. This Christmas tea is for you."

Stepping into the bakery, Lynne saw rows of angel food cakes directly in front of her. And not the tube kind either, the loaf kind. "These were the lightest, fluffiest, best-looking angel food cakes I'd ever seen," she recalled later. Then she counted; there were seventeen of them. "Thank you, Lord," she said silently. "Do you have any more?" she asked the clerk.

"Yes, we do," came the reply. "Normally we don't carry this kind. In fact, they arrived just a few minutes ago and I only had time to put these out. I'll get the others for you."

Lynne loaded her car with angel food loaf cakes. On arriving home, she began working. At ten o'clock at night, she finished her work, and only then did she begin counting. She had exactly 220 angel food jelly rolls. In amazement, she recalls, "Not one too many. Not one shy."

Certainly God has better things to do than cater Christmas teas. We have a world full of serious needs. But remember that our God baby-sits sparrows and counts the hairs on our heads. The Bible consistently shows him as God of the great *and* the ordinary. Perhaps the greatest miracle in this story was the confirmation of his love and care for this new believer, Lynne Hall.

"God sent me those angel food cakes from heaven," she says. "Just as surely as God is involved in any miracle, I know he was involved in mine. I am not the same person I was back then; my life is filled with a sense of peace that only a faith in God can bring. God's love can be found in the tiniest of details."

> I can do no great things, Lord. But I can do a few small things with great love.
> Marilyn Morgan Helleberg

Send Us a Hot Water Bottle This Afternoon, Lord

Cambridge to Congo—quite a step for Helen Roseveare. After receiving her medical training at England's prestigious Cambridge University, she went to Central Africa to establish a medical center for the Worldwide Evangelization for Christ (WEC)

93

> We ought to act with God in the greatest simplicity, talking to Him frankly and plainly, and fervently asking His help in all that we do and right while we're doing what we do.
>
> Brother Lawrence

in 1953. Her new home, then called Belgian Congo (later Zaire, and then simply Congo), was rife with rebellion, poverty, and illness. Dr. Roseveare's posh training hardly prepared her for all the obstacles she would face.

One night in the labor ward, she worked to save the life of a young mother and her tiny premature baby. Despite Dr. Roseveare's efforts, the mother died. The baby was in critical condition; in addition, the baby's two-year-old sister needed care. Because the medical clinic had no electricity, it had no incubator.

The nights got chilly at that time of year, and the doctor knew the baby would have to be kept warm somehow. A nurse was sent to stoke the fire and fill a hot water bottle. When she returned, Dr. Roseveare realized from the look on the nurse's face that they had a serious problem. "The hot water bottle burst," the nurse sobbed, "and it is our last hot water bottle!"

That night Dr. Roseveare told the nurse to sleep close to the baby, near the fire, but not too near, and out of drafts from windows and doors. The baby survived the night but was still in critical condition.

The next day, as usual, Dr. Roseveare met with the children of the clinic's orphanage for prayer and Bible reading. Asking them to pray for the tiny baby, she spoke of the need for a hot water bottle. If the baby got chills, it would die very quickly.

During the prayer time, a ten-year-old girl named Ruth prayed earnestly, "Please, God, send us a water bottle. It'll be no good tomorrow, God, as the baby'll be dead, so please send it this afternoon. And while you are at it, would you please send a dolly for her little sister so she'll know you really love her."

Dr. Roseveare didn't know if she should really add her "amen" to the girl's prayer or not. God could answer prayer, but this bordered on the ridiculous. In Dr. Roseveare's words, "The only way God could answer this particular prayer would be by sending me a parcel from the homeland. I had been in Africa for

94

almost four years at that time, and I had never, ever received a parcel from home; anyway, if anyone did send me a parcel, who would put in a hot water bottle? I lived on the equator."

That afternoon as the doctor was teaching a class at the nurses' training school, she received word that a car was in front of her home. When she got there, the car had gone, but on the porch was a twenty-two-pound parcel.

She couldn't believe it. She sent for some of the orphanage children to help her open it. The box was packed with a variety of things, and the children clustered around as each item was pulled out. Knitted jerseys, knitted bandages for leprosy patients, a box of mixed raisins and sultanas. Then the doctor put her hand in the box and pulled out the next item. Yes, it was . . . a brand new rubber hot water bottle.

The doctor was in tears—she had not believed that God could do it. Ruth, the ten-year-old who had prayed for this, was now standing very close to the box, but she wasn't satisfied yet. "If God has sent the bottle, he must have sent the dolly for the baby's sister too."

So Dr. Roseveare continued to rummage in the box, and finally, from the bottom of the box, she pulled out a small beautifully dressed dolly.

The package had been mailed by Dr. Roseveare's former Sunday school class in England and had been en route for five months, arriving a couple of hours after Ruth had prayed. Why did someone send a hot water bottle to the equator? Apparently, someone was in tune with God's prompting.

Following a Little Bird

With a name like Goforth, they *had* to be missionaries. Jonathan and Rosalind Goforth served in China, Manchuria, and Korea early in the twentieth century. In fact, Jonathan has been called China's greatest missionary evangelist. Revivals begun under the Goforths' ministry made a lasting impression on mission work in these countries, and some experts trace back to the

> "Look at the birds of the air; they do not sow or reap or store away in barns, and yet your heavenly Father feeds them. Are you not much more valuable than they?"
>
> Matthew 6:26

Goforths the spirit of prayer and piety that has characterized the Christian church in Korea ever since.

Rosalind Goforth was noted for her prayer ministry. A little book that she wrote, *How I Know God Answers Prayer,* is filled with stories of how God answered prayer for them in their ministry.

Where did she get her interest in prayer? From an earlier missionary—Hudson Taylor, founder of the China Inland Mission. Before she became a missionary, just before she married Jonathan, Rosalind read a book by Taylor and was impressed with the answers to prayer he received. What made it special was that he didn't ask anyone but God to meet his need—and God did.

As Rosalind prepared for marriage, she was embarrassed that she was fifty dollars in debt, and she didn't want to saddle her husband-to-be with that indebtedness. "If you cannot trust God for this," she chided herself, "are you worthy of being a missionary?" When no financial help came, she was tempted to tell others of her need, but she didn't. Then the night before her wedding, fellow workers presented her with a purse. Opening the purse, she found a check for fifty dollars. Rosalind felt it was God's seal on her new life.

Rosalind's belief in the power of prayer began in childhood, with a story about her grandfather that she heard from her mother. When her grandfather was just a boy, he visited cousins who lived near a dense forest. One day when he and the cousins went out picking wildflowers, they became hopelessly lost in the forest. For a while they tried to find their way out, but they couldn't. By this time they all were crying.

Then the oldest cousin, a girl, said, "When Mother died, she told us to always tell Jesus if we were in any trouble. Let's kneel down and ask him to take us home."

So the three little children knelt down and prayed in the forest. When they opened their eyes, one of them noticed a little bird, apparently quite tame. It was so close to them that the children could almost touch it. As a child reached, the bird hopped away, and the children started following. The bird kept hopping and flying in front of the children. Then suddenly it flew into the air and away. When the children looked up, they found themselves on the edge of the woods, and there in the distance was their home.

Rosalind Goforth never forgot her grandfather's story. She and her husband suffered greatly in China's Boxer Rebellion of 1900 and endured great challenges in Manchuria and Korea, but the story of the little bird was never forgotten.

She writes, "It is not surprising that I came even as a very little child to just 'tell Jesus' when in trouble." Then she would expect God's amazing answers.

Blue Coats and a Flashing Blue Light

Winter was coming. In the mile-high city of Denver, that would mean snow and cold.

No news flash there, except it created a problem for Lyn Behrens, who had just moved from southern California to do some research while on sabbatical from a teaching job. She had two young daughters and very little money. Her girls would need warm coats.

Whenever she could, Lyn took the girls to the shopping malls to look for winter garb, specifically winter coats, but she could find nothing that would fit her budget and her girls' sizes. When Denver's first snowfall hit, she knew she would have to do something for her girls. So they went to a Kmart on the south side of the city. Certainly Kmart would have something she could afford. In the children's clothing section, she thought she had found what she had been looking for—all-weather coats, sky blue, lined with removable flannel—and Kmart had one left of each size needed by her daughters. *Thank you, Lord.*

When she looked at the price tag, her praise turned to panic. The coats cost far more than Lyn could afford. She had money

Father, let others read Your handwriting across my life today.

Elizabeth Sherrill

to buy one of the coats, but not both. So, which of her girls would shiver through the winter?

Kmart had no other options. Nearly in tears, Lyn drove her daughters to the local Target store. There they found absolutely nothing that fit.

Back in the car, she talked to the Lord. *What should I do, Lord? The girls have to have coats; it's not a luxury, it's a need.*

She then began rehearsing the events of the past several months. It was a major move to come to Denver, and she thought she had been following the Lord's direction in doing it. Had she been wrong about it? This was the place where she needed to do her research during her sabbatical, wasn't it? Or was it a selfish move on her part? Lyn struggled with self-doubt.

Disappointed and distressed, Lyn headed home. What could she do? On the way, they passed Kmart again, and she decided to drive into the parking lot. By this time, her girls didn't want to spend any more time in useless shopping. "Let's get home," they urged her.

But Lyn parked the car in the parking lot and prayed. Then she remembered a verse in the third chapter of Malachi. It promised that if a person is faithful in giving his tithes to the Lord, the Lord will "throw open the floodgates of heaven and pour out so much blessing that you will not have room enough for it." In spite of her tight budget, she had continued to be faithful in her giving, so in the car outside of Kmart she prayed again, claiming God's promise to open the floodgates of heaven.

She wasn't sure what the Lord would do, but she and her daughters got out of the car and walked into the store. Almost immediately they heard the tinny voice on the speaker system announcing a "new blue-light special" in the children's department. It didn't take them long to find the flashing blue light—just above the coats they had looked at two hours earlier. The special was: "Two coats for the price of one."

Wasting no time, they grabbed the coats and rushed to the checkout line. By the time they had completed their purchase, the five-minute blue-light special had ended.

Lyn and her daughters were amazed at God's miraculous timing and his concern about the ordinary things of their lives.

All of that happened in 1981, and a few years later, B. Lyn Behrens was named president of Loma Linda University, back in southern California.

Exactly Five Pounds of Potatoes

Kenneth and Suzie Ware were flat broke. But at least they were together and still alive.

When World War II erupted, the Wares were living in France. Kenneth Ware was an evangelist well-known throughout the country; Suzie was an artist with some of her portraits hanging in the Louvre. After the Nazis invaded the country, the Wares' home became a haven for Jewish refugees. But since Kenneth and Suzie were both public figures, the Nazis were watching them closely.

Suzie bore a son, and for the safety of their child they knew they would have to flee the country. In the process, Kenneth was arrested and beaten, but one German guard, discovering he was a preacher, released him. In September they arrived in Lausanne, Switzerland, safe and sound and flat broke.

Suzie would never forget the September Saturday morning when she prayed very specifically for groceries. "God," she prayed, "I need five pounds of potatoes, two pounds of pastry flour, apples, pears, a cauliflower, carrots, veal cutlets for Saturday, and beef for Sunday."

It was a tall order, considering how short of funds they were.

Early that afternoon, someone knocked at the Wares' door. Outside was a man with a basket of groceries. She didn't recognize him but guessed he was between thirty and forty. He wore a long blue apron over his work clothes.

"Mrs. Ware," he called her by name, "I'm bringing you what you asked for." She listened to him speak. He spoke in French, but without the Swiss accent of most Lausanne residents.

Suzie was flustered. "I . . . I . . . I have not ordered anything. There must be a mistake." She called for her husband, Kenneth, who came to the door. "There are twenty-five apartments here in this complex, sir. Are you sure you have the right one?" he asked the man.

The deliveryman seemed to ignore the question. Instead he repeated, "Mrs. Ware, I am bringing you what you asked for." Without pausing, he carried the basket into the kitchen, emptying the contents on the kitchen table.

What amazed Suzie was that the items on her table were not only the exact items for which she had prayed in the morning but also the exact amounts: five pounds of potatoes, for instance. Suzie was dumbstruck. After the man left, they looked out their window to see him exit the building; maybe his truck or delivery car would be by the curb. But they didn't see him leave the building, and there was no vehicle in front.

After the war, the Wares went back to Paris to work with refugees. They fed, clothed, taught, and brought the gospel to thousands, and they always kept looking for that Lausanne deliveryman, but without success.

Honey, Go Buy Those Bluebonnets

To celebrate their thirtieth wedding anniversary, Jeanie and Martus Miley wanted a painting to mount over their fireplace. What kind of painting? Well, they were Texans, and Texas is known as the Bluebonnet State, so they thought a picture showing a field of bluebonnets would be perfect.

This wouldn't just be an expression of state pride. It would also remind them of how God had brought them through difficult times in the previous five years. At times during those years, they had felt that God seemed far away, and they had struggled through several "dark nights of the soul." But things were looking better now, and they were rejoicing again in God's goodness and grace.

> Father, help me not to waste time by being forever busy. Amen.
>
> Scott Walker

So on their anniversary, Jeanie headed for a souvenir shop and found a watercolor print they could afford. Martus, who usually acquiesced to Jeanie's taste in such matters, said, "That isn't nearly good enough." He took her instead to an art gallery, where he pointed to a bluebonnet painting by W. A. Slaughter, a well-known Texas artist. Both of them loved it, but Jeanie knew it was out of their price bracket.

So they didn't buy a painting on their anniversary. Nothing else measured up to the Slaughter work.

Then throughout the year, things became more difficult again. Jeanie's mother died, other factors added to their stress, and for some reason they again felt that God was distant.

Through it all, they couldn't put the bluebonnet painting out of their minds. As they approached their thirty-first anniversary, they kept thinking about it. They could probably afford the painting, but it seemed frivolous to spend such a sum on themselves. Jeanie wished that her mom and dad were still around so she could ask their permission to buy it. Of course, she and Martus were both well into adulthood, but somewhere deep inside her, she felt she needed her parents' approval for such an extravagant purchase.

They went to another art gallery in another town to look over other paintings by Slaughter. And again they saw bluebonnets in his paintings. But these works were just as expensive.

That night, as the couple prayed together, Jeanie said, "O God, please ask my mom and dad if it's okay for me to buy that painting." Martus laughed at her, and she laughed too. But if her parents wouldn't give her a go-ahead, then God would have to do it himself, she felt.

The next day they returned to the art gallery and saw what Jeanie thought was "the most beautiful bluebonnet painting

101

ever." They retreated to a nearby coffee shop to discuss their decision. And there, in that shop, sat one of her father's old friends. Jeanie had not seen him in years. They explained their quest for a bluebonnet painting, and he updated them on his life. Then Jeanie and Martus took a table in a corner to talk about the painting. They finally decided to buy it, but Jeanie was still a bit uneasy. She wished God could confirm that decision in some way.

On their way out of the coffee shop, they stopped to say goodbye to her father's old friend. He took Jeanie by the hand and said, "Honey, go buy those bluebonnets. That would make your mother and daddy so happy."

It was the confirmation Jeanie needed.

Was it a coincidence? Jeanie doesn't think so. She feels that "the one who cared about the lilies of the fields also cared about bluebonnets and grown-up children who needed some gladness in the midst of the winter."

8

Everyone Talks about the Weather, But . . .

Miracles regarding Nature

> Elijah was a man just like us. He prayed earnestly that it would not rain, and it did not rain on the land for three and a half years. Again he prayed, and the heavens gave rain, and the earth produced its crops.
>
> James 5:17–18

Everyone talks about the weather, but no one does anything about it. That's an old witticism, but there are exceptions, as we shall see. When you're on speaking terms with the one who makes the weather, sometimes you *can* do something about it. Astonishing but true.

We should tread carefully here. The ballplayer's boon is the farmer's bane. Pray for clear skies for the Sunday school picnic and the crops might go dry. Pray for rain and the tuna casserole gets soggy. You'll read several stories here about the effects of weather on war. Does that mean God is on one side or the other? We can see him allying against the genocidal Nazis, but were the French really that bad?

Several of these accounts harken back to Elijah. You remember the prophet challenging the idolaters on Mount Carmel. It was a classic showdown—winner take all. Which god will make it rain? It seems that our God often works miracles to prove himself. He did so in Elijah's day and he keeps doing so today. Astonishing but true.

Almighty God, amid all the storms and troubles of life, may we rest in you. All things are under your care, governed by your will, and guarded by your love. With a quiet heart, may we rejoice that the darkness and the light are both alike to you.

George Dawson (adapted)

The Pilgrims' Weather Report

The weather report wasn't good. In fact, it hadn't been good for weeks.

The year was 1623, and the Pilgrims were facing their third summer in the New World. During their second summer, they had not planted enough, and they suffered for it in the fall and winter. This year they knew they needed at least twice as great a yield as they had their first year. So the Pilgrim leaders asked all the settlers to do a second planting.

Some time after the second planting, however, a dry spell lengthened into a drought. Week after week for twelve weeks, the Pilgrims looked for rain, which never came. Even the most elderly of the Native Americans could remember nothing like it.

Pilgrim leader Edward Winslow graphically described the condition of the corn plants: "Both blade and stalk hanging the head and changing the color in such manner as we judged it utterly dead. . . . Now were our hopes overthrown, and we discouraged, our joy turned into mourning . . . because God, which hitherto had been our only shield and supporter, now seemed in his anger to arm Himself against us." The drought, Winslow reported, forced individuals to examine their relationships with God, but the people also made a corporate move "to humble ourselves together before the Lord by fasting and prayer. To that end, a day was appointed by public authority and set apart from all other employments."

> Units of prayer combined, like drops of water, make an ocean which defies resistance.
>
> Frank Laubach

So the Pilgrims gathered together for a prayer meeting. Winslow continued:

But O the mercy of our God who was as ready to hear as we were to ask! For though in the morning, when we assembled together, the heavens were as clear and the drought as like to continue as it ever was, yet (our exercise continuing some eight or nine hours) before our departure, the weather was overcast, the clouds gathered on all sides. On the next morning distilled such soft, sweet and moderate showers of rain, continuing some fourteen days and mixed with such seasonable weather, as it was hard to say whether our withered corn or our drooping affections were most quickened or revived, such was the bounty and goodness of our God!

Two weeks of rain in answer to the Pilgrims' prayers! Another Pilgrim leader, William Bradford, confirmed it: "It came, without either wind or thunder, or any violence, and by degrees in that abundance as that the earth was thoroughly wet and soaked therewith. Which did so apparently revive and quicken the decayed corn and other fruits, as was wonderful to see and made the Indians astonished to behold."

Winslow added that the Indians admired "the goodeness of our God towards us, that wrought so great a change in so short a time, showing the difference between their conjurations and our invocation on the name of God for rain."

The yield that year was so abundant that the Pilgrims ended up with a surplus of corn, which they used in trading that winter with Native Americans north of them who had not had a good growing season. Two years earlier, they had enjoyed a Thanksgiving celebration with the local tribespeople after their first harvest, and now they scheduled another one. Native chief Massasoit was again the guest of honor, and this time he brought his principal wife, three other leaders, and 120 braves. Fortunately he again brought venison and turkey as well.

The second Thanksgiving may have surpassed the first one.

Astrup's Rain

It was a challenge worthy of Elijah. Could the missionary make it rain?

John Astrup, serving among the Zulus in Africa, had been trying for years to set up a church and school in a particular area, but the king of that territory refused to grant permission. Contemptuous of Christianity, the Zulu king said the tribal witch doctors were good enough for him.

Then came 1904, and a disastrous drought. The heat in the valleys of the Tugela River hit 145 degrees. Vegetation burned to a crisp. Farmland baked. Crops shriveled. Although the witch doctors danced, pranced, and shook their rattles, they could get no rain out of the heavens.

Finally the Zulu king sent a delegation to missionary Astrup. Would he come and pray to his God for rain? He agreed to, asking that the whole tribe be assembled for mass prayer.

Early the next morning, Astrup descended twenty-five hundred feet into the valley, walking through snake-infested bush and wading across what remained of the Tugela River, now full of starving crocodiles. In the village he faced more than two thousand Zulus. He could see hunger on their faces. When he announced that he would pray, he was surprised to see all two thousand of them throw themselves down into the dust. Astrup prayed, asking God to send rain and help the Zulu people in their distress. He finished his prayer, as he often did in his church services, with the Lord's Prayer. Then from the ground, he was surprised to hear the muffled voices of the bowed Zulus repeating phrases from that prayer.

> Think we, like some weak prince, th' Eternal Cause Prone for his fav'rites to reverse his laws? When the loose mountain trembles from on high, Shall gravitation cease, if you go by?
>
> Alexander Pope

Nothing happened. No rains came; no clouds appeared in the sky. Astrup said good-bye and then climbed up a mountain range before pausing for a rest. While resting, he heard the sound of thunder behind him. Turning around, he saw an amazing sight. Above the king's dwelling and the Zulu settlement, dark clouds were gathering. Lightning flashed, and rain began to fall. Soon a tremendous torrent came, but only on that one area.

About three months later, another Zulu delegation came to visit the missionary. They announced that their old king had died. His son was now in charge, and he and the rest of the Zulus wanted to know how to give thanks to God for the marvelous rain.

When Astrup returned for the thanksgiving service, the grass was now four to five feet high. Shrubs were flowering and trees were branching out. But that wasn't all that would grow in these now-fertile fields. The following week, a church and school were started.

Why the French Invasion Never Happened

Revival was blazing through America in the 1740s. George Whitefield was preaching up a storm, winning converts wherever he went, and Jonathan Edwards was calling for repentance

> Providence is God's ordering all issues and events of things, after the counsel of His will, to His own glory.
>
> Thomas Watson

from his Massachusetts pulpit. Historians have called it the Great Awakening.

Other activities were going on as well. The British colonies in America were facing a serious assault from the French.

In June 1746, the French Grand Fleet, consisting of seventy ships and eight thousand soldiers under the command of Duc d'Anville, had eluded a British blockade and was headed for the American colonies. The French were determined to destroy every British-American settlement in the New World.

Colonial Christians, aware of their danger, asked God to protect them from the invasion. Up and down the seacoast, churches conducted prayer meetings asking for divine intervention on their behalf. This might not have happened a decade earlier, but during the Great Awakening, people were learning to turn to God.

So what happened?

First, the French fleet, relying on the winds, was delayed by a prolonged calm. When wind finally came up, it developed into a fierce storm with severe lightning; several ships were disabled. Next, a plague broke out among the sailors and soldiers. Some thirteen hundred died. More storms came, scattering the entire fleet. By the end of August, only fifty-three ships remained. Then another storm came near the island of Sable, and several more ships were stranded.

So only a portion of the French fleet reached Halifax, Nova Scotia. There Duc d'Anville expected to meet with a squadron of French ships coming from the West Indies. But the squadron, which had arrived several weeks earlier, had given up on the arrival of Duc d'Anville's armada and decided to return to France.

Soon after the duke arrived in Halifax, he became deeply depressed by the entire unbelievable situation. Much of his fleet was lost; many of his surviving troops were sick and dying. The duke also became ill, and on September 10 he died. His second in command attempted suicide.

Misfortunes continued, but the French were determined to invade the East Coast in spite of everything. Although another thousand men died of disease in September, a new commander gave the order to sail on October 13.

> The hour of prayer is like the Gulf Stream, imparting warmth to all that is cold.
>
> Abraham Joshua Heschel

Not knowing all that had gone on before, New Englanders set aside October 16 as a day of prayer and fasting, asking God to deliver them from the coming siege. The colonists could see the French ships hovering off the coast. As a New England pastor described it, "Never [was] prayer more prevalent, than on this occasion. A prayer-hearing God stretched forth the arm of his power and destroyed that mighty armament in a manner almost as extraordinary as the drowning of Pharaoh and his host in the Red Sea."

On October 15, the day before the designated day of prayer, another violent storm hit the French fleet, scattering and damaging more ships. On the sixteenth, the weather improved, and the French tried to bring their armada together again. But that evening, after another storm ravaged the fleet, the remaining ships gave up their plans and staggered back to France.

The Christians Carried Umbrellas

It seemed that no one could make it rain.

One summer in the early 1900s in northern Nigeria, the crops were failing from the lack of rain. Starvation was imminent.

The tribespeople tried everything they knew to get rain from the heavens. They beat their drums, blew their horns, and screamed and shouted to their gods. At the end of a week, they sacrificed a calf, then drank the blood and ate the raw flesh. Still there was no rain.

The Muslims in the area were next to call for rain. Confidently they told the tribal chief, "We will bring the rain." If noise could have done it, they would have brought the heavens down. They screamed and cried three times a day and three times at

109

> We begin to live secretly with God in an invisible world, whose resources become more real to us than the visible.
>
> Norman Grubb

night. They fasted and then sacrificed a lamb. Still no rains came.

After church one Sunday, an African pastor came to Thomas Titcombe, a pioneer missionary with the Sudan Interior Mission. The pastor asked, "Isn't it time for us to pray for rain? Our people pray to idols that cannot see, hear, or speak. They can't help us. The Muslims pray to Allah, but Mohammed lived and then died. Allah and Mohammed cannot help us. But Jesus came out of the grave and said, 'All power is given unto me.' Yes, I think it is time for us to pray."

So the next night, missionary Titcombe and the local pastor called for a prayer meeting for rain. When the church bell rang to call worshipers to the church, not a cloud was in the sky.

Titcombe walked into the church and smiled at what he saw. On one side were seated the Muslims and the animistic tribespeople. On the other side sat the Christians, and all the Christians had open umbrellas over their heads.

Umbrellas? Before the missionary could ask, the Christians told him their reasoning: "We have come to pray for rain, and didn't you tell us that only those who believe God answers prayer were to come?" The umbrellas over their heads were their sign of faith that God would answer their prayer.

When it came time for the Christians to pray, their prayer was simply, "Lord, we need rain." One by one, they prayed much the same thing. Soon they heard the tapping of raindrops on the corrugated roof.

Missionary Titcombe didn't have to say a word. The new Christians in Nigeria had taught him a lesson he would never forget about the meaning of faith.

When you pray for rain, don't forget your umbrella.

How God Answered Prayer on D-Day

It may have been the largest invasion force in the history of the world. Some 250,000 men, 1,400 aircraft, 3,300 assault ships,

6 battleships, and countless destroyers were poised to invade Europe. The day was June 6, 1944. Few who were alive at the time will ever forget.

> Prayer is the only power in the world that seems to overcome the so-called laws of nature.
>
> Dr. Alexis Carrel

The D-Day invasion was crucial to the outcome of World War II— a must-win battle.

Everyone knew the invasion was imminent, but no one knew the exact time or place. President Franklin D. Roosevelt called on Americans to pray. Some had asked for a day of prayer, but the president said, "Because the road is long and the desire is great, I ask that our people devote themselves in a continuance of prayer."

King George VI called on the entire British Empire to pray: "We are not unmindful of our own shortcomings, past and present. We shall ask not that God may do our will, but that we may be called to do the will of God."

As the day approached, General George Dempsey, commander of the British and Canadian forces, met in the parish church in Portsdown, England, with four hundred officers and men and prayed for an hour in what he called "one of the most moving experiences of my life."

June 5 was supposed to be D-Day, the day of the momentous invasion, but hazardous weather delayed it. General Dwight D. Eisenhower later explained what happened:

> The final conference for determining the feasibility of attacking on June 5 was scheduled at 4:00 A.M. on June 4. . . . Some of the attacking contingents had already been ordered to sea. . . . On the morning of June 4 the report we received was discouraging. Low clouds, high winds, and formidable wave action were predicted to make landing a most hazardous affair. The meteorologists said that air support would be impossible, naval gunfire would be inefficient, and even the handling of small boats would be rendered difficult.
>
> At 3:30 the next morning our little tent was shaking and shuddering under a wind of almost hurricane proportions. It seemed impossible that in such conditions there was any reason for even discussing the situation. . . . If we had persisted in the attempt

111

Prayer works results beyond the individual himself, both in the physical and the spiritual world.

William W. Patton

to land on June 5, a major disaster would almost surely have resulted.

According to the Allied weathermen, they could expect about thirty-six hours of good weather to begin on June 6, and then another spell of bad weather. Eisenhower quickly announced the decision to go ahead with the attack on June 6.

As dawn approached on June 6, the winds were still at near-hurricane proportions. In the midst of such winds, an attack would end in certain defeat.

Eisenhower recalled: "I made the most agonizing decision of my life." Should he delay again? He would have to wait two weeks for the tidal conditions to be right again for an invasion. He decided to go ahead. "If there were nothing else in my life to prove the existence of an almighty and merciful God, the events of the next twenty-four hours did it."

Suddenly the weather changed, the D-Day invasion of Europe proceeded, and loss of life was far below what had been anticipated.

Inside Europe, the Nazi commanders also consulted their weathermen. The German generals were told that an invasion would be impossible under the weather conditions. As a result, many of the high-ranking German officers, including General Erwin Rommel, went to a birthday party.

By the way, if the Allies had waited until June 18 to attempt the invasion, they would have encountered the worst storm to hit the English Channel in eighty years.

George Müller in a Fog

Imagine this: Someone knocks on your door and asks, "Do you want any money?"

That happened to George Müller of Bristol, England. In fact, that sort of thing often happened to George Müller. Even at the tender age of twenty-five, he believed that he should ask only God, and not other people, for whatever he needed.

His policy was tested early, since Müller and his young wife were nearly broke. But they prayed about it—and four hours later, a woman knocked on the door offering money.

The problem was, Müller had promised to tell only the Lord about his financial needs, so how was he to answer the woman at the door?

The woman persisted, "But the Lord has told me to give you some money."

So Müller accepted what she offered as an answer to his prayers. At the time he had no idea that he and his wife would start an orphanage in a few years and that he would eventually have to feed more than two thousand children every day at the orphanage— without ever asking a person for money. His faith for God's provision is almost legendary.

Müller's faith in other areas, however, is not so well-known. After he reached seventy years of age, he began traveling internationally, telling others about God's faithfulness to him and his orphanage ministry. Once as he was crossing the Atlantic, his ship encountered a deep fog. The captain of the ship later told this story:

> Sometimes a fog will settle over a vessel's deck and yet leave the topmast clear. Then a sailor goes up aloft and gets a lookout which the helmsman on deck cannot get. So prayer sends the soul aloft, lifts it above the clouds in which our selfishness and egotism befog us, and gives us a chance to see which way to steer.
>
> Thomas W. Handford

We had a man of God on board, George Müller of Bristol. I had been on the bridge for twenty-two hours and never left it. I was startled by someone tapping me on the shoulder. It was Müller.

"Captain, I have come to tell you I must be in Quebec on Saturday afternoon."

"Impossible!" I exclaimed.

"I have never broken an engagement in fifty years," he replied.

I answered, "I am willing, but I am helpless. We are in a fog—"

On the day the LORD gave the Amorites over to Israel, Joshua said to the LORD in the presence of Israel:

"O sun, stand still over Gibeon,

O moon, over the Valley of Aijalon. . . ."

The sun stopped in the middle of the sky and delayed going down about a full day. There has never been a day like it before or since, a day when the LORD listened to a man. Surely the LORD was fighting for Israel!

Joshua 10:12–14

"Let us go down to the chart room and pray," said George Müller.

I looked at him, and I thought to myself, what lunatic asylum could the man have come from? I never heard of such a thing.

I said, "Mr. Müller, do you know how dense the fog is?"

"No," he replied, "my eye is not on the density of the fog, but on the living God who controls every circumstance of my life." He got down on his knees and prayed a most simple prayer. "O, Lord, if it is consistent with Thy will, please remove this fog in five minutes. Thou knowest the engagement Thou made for me in Quebec for Saturday. I believe it is Thy will."

When he finished, I was going to pray, but he put his hand on my shoulder and told me not to pray. "First, you do not believe He will; and second, I believe He has, and there is no need to pray."

According to the ship captain, the fog lifted just as Müller had requested. But the weather wasn't the only thing that cleared up that day. The captain also reported that the event "completely revolutionized the whole of my life."

Watchman Nee and the Island of Mei-Hwa

Opposed by a powerful Communist regime, Watchman Nee inspired millions of Chinese Christians. Though he was arrested in 1952 and died in prison in 1972, his "little flock" movement spawned thousands of house churches in China. Today Watchman Nee is still remembered worldwide for his devotional books such as *The Normal Christian Life* and *Sit, Walk, Stand*.

114

Shortly after his conversion, when he was just seventeen, Nee and six other enthusiastic young Christians sailed to a small island and a fishing village called Mei-hwa, in an effort to convert the entire island for Christ. The young evangelists worked hard but saw no converts.

Every year on January 11, a great festival was held to honor the local god, To-Wang. The villagers proudly told the Christian evangelists that it had not rained on the annual festival for 286 years. When he heard this, one of Watchman Nee's associates, Kuo-ching Lee, impulsively challenged the villagers: "I promise you, our God, who is the true God, will make it rain on January 11."

> God supersedes natural law and he has ordained that prayer shall be one of the causes that occasions his divine intervention in which he transcends his own natural laws for higher purposes.
>
> Harold Lindsell

The crowd laughed at him. Yet they agreed to listen to these young men if it did rain on that date.

When Watchman Nee heard what Kuo-ching had done, he was bothered. In fact, he was planning to rebuke his associate but instead decided to pray about it. "Father, have we gone too far? Should we leave this village now before your name is disgraced?" Then he remembered a phrase from the Old Testament book of 2 Kings: "Where is the LORD God of Elijah?" He recalled the contest that Elijah had with the prophets of Baal on Mount Carmel, and he thought that maybe God intended to do something similar in the little village of Mei-hwa.

Instead of rebuking Kuo-ching, Watchman Nee instructed his associates to tell everyone in the village about the challenge. The God of Elijah would send rain on January 11. The entire village soon got the message; excitement spread throughout the area.

But when Watchman Nee woke up on January 11, it didn't look good for the Christians. The sun was shining brightly in a cloudless sky. At breakfast, Watchman Nee and his companions prayed, "Father, please accept our prayer as a gentle reminder." Before Nee had finished praying, a few drops of rain began falling on the tiled roof. Soon it was a downpour.

When the storm stopped, the area priest announced he had made a big mistake about the date. The celebration was to have taken place this year on January 14, not on January 11.

In the next three days, the seven Christians continued not only praying but also spreading the message of Christ, and within those three days, thirty villagers became Christians.

The weather on January 14 was almost a duplicate of the weather on the eleventh. Once again a huge storm struck Mei-hwa in the morning hours. In the following weeks, a church was established on the island, and the grip of the pagan religion was broken.

For Watchman Nee, Kuo-ching Lee, and the others, it was dramatic proof that the God who lived in Elijah's time is still the same today.

9

Lost Sheep and the Searching Shepherd

Remarkable Conversion Stories in Answer to Prayer

And this is my prayer: that your love may abound more and more in knowledge and depth of insight, so that you may be able to discern what is best and may be pure and blameless until the day of Christ.

Philippians 1:9–10

What is conversion? The word itself speaks of a turning, a changing, a transformation. It is one of many words we Christians use for the beginning of a relationship with God through Jesus Christ. A person "gets saved" or "repents" or "finds Christ" or "makes a decision for Christ." The theological words include *redemption, justification,* and *reconciliation.* The Bible speaks often of this moment, using all these words and more. Simply put, the person who is "in Christ" becomes a "new creation; the old has gone, the new has come!" (2 Cor. 5:17).

Some disagreements exist about the precise nature of this moment. Are certain elements required in a "prayer for salvation"? Is there always a single moment of redemption, or do people sometimes ease into it? Do you really "find Christ" or does Christ find you? We will let the scholars bicker over the details, but we know this: It's good to pray for people to know Christ.

We can surely pray this with confidence, knowing that God wants relationships with people. We can pray for the wooing and convicting that God's Spirit can do in people's hearts. Remember that God often uses us to help answer our own prayers. If you're asking God to save your neighbor, consider what things you might do or say to advance that cause.

> *Jesus, what didst Thou find in me*
> *That Thou hast dealt so lovingly?*
> *How great the joy that Thou has brought*
> *So far exceeding hope or thought.*
>
> Henry Collins

The Face in the Photo Section

Steve Davis hadn't prayed in years. He didn't have much time for praying now. He was busy as a flight instructor at his own flight school, with three airplanes of his own. And he was still only twenty-three.

He remembered when he used to pray, years ago when Christianity seemed real to him. But that was far away and years ago.

Now a feeling of sadness gripped him; perhaps his own lack of faith saddened him. So he prayed for the first time in years, and his prayer went something like this: "Now, wait a minute,

God. Something tells me you're not real. I'd really like to know you the way I thought I did. I want to have the faith I used to have. But I just can't blindly accept that stuff I grew up with. If you'll let me know that you're real, I will serve you, but I've got to know. I can't pretend."

He was surprised that he didn't feel anything special after he prayed. He thought that if God really existed, and if God really cared, something unusual would happen.

Steve Davis had been raised in Mexico, where his dad was a missionary pilot. He admired his dad, who had instilled in him a love for flying. In fact, Steve had wanted to be a missionary pilot when he grew up, just like his dad.

His parents had given him a book to read, *Through Gates of Splendor* by Elisabeth Elliot. It told the story of five missionaries who were killed by Indians in Ecuador in 1956. Steve was captivated by the life of the missionary pilot, Nate Saint, who lost his life with the others. At times in his childhood, Steve imagined himself as Nate Saint, flying into the South American jungles.

But in his later teen years, he had doubts about Christianity, so he stopped thinking about it. His life went on, but he began to recognize an emptiness within. That's when he decided to try praying again—one more time. But apparently without success.

Then he came across his old copy of *Through Gates of Splendor.* In the middle of the book was a photo section, and one of the photos portrayed Nate Saint's son. Steve remembered the strange kinship he had felt with that boy. After all, they were both sons of missionary pilots. And, doing the math, he figured that Nate Saint's son was probably just about his own age. Now, glancing over that old book, he began to wonder if Nate Saint's son had also lost his faith.

One day at the airstrip from which he conducted his flight instruction, he was thinking about all of this when suddenly he heard an airplane engine. It was raining hard, but there was a Cessna 172 dropping out of the sky toward the runway. A little

> We begin praying for others by first quieting our fleshly activity and listening to the silent thunder of the Lord of hosts.
>
> Richard J. Foster

later the pilot and passenger came in, dripping wet, asking if there was a motel nearby.

When Steve turned to one of the Hispanic workers and relayed the question in Spanish, the visiting pilot entered into the Spanish conversation.

"Where did you learn such good Spanish?" Steve asked.

The pilot replied, "My parents were missionaries in Ecuador. I grew up there."

Ecuador? Steve asked if he had heard of any of the five missionary martyrs who were mentioned in the book. The plane's passenger said delicately, "One of them was his dad."

Yes, this pilot was Nate Saint's son, the one Steve Davis had identified with as a child. It turned out that he was also named Steve.

Was this just a coincidence? Or had God amazingly answered his prayer? Steve Davis didn't know, but he invited Steve Saint and the passenger to stay with him for the night and save the cost of a motel.

They talked far into the night. Steve Davis had many questions, but it seemed that Nate Saint's son had answers to all of them. "I knew that God had answered my prayer in the most personal, loving way possible," Steve Davis now says. "Again I had a joy inside."

The NAACP and the Klan

"I'm going to love you and pray for you whether you like it or not."

That was the gauntlet thrown down by Wade Watts, state president of the Oklahoma NAACP. He was talking to Johnny Lee Clary, Grand Dragon of the Oklahoma Ku Klux Klan.

It was 1979, and a Tulsa radio program had invited them to debate. Before the show, Watts put out his hand; Clary refused to shake it. Watts was a black man with a worn Bible under his arm. Clary had just turned twenty but already had become Grand Dragon for the state KKK.

Watts reached out his hand a second time. This time he reached Clary's hand and shook it. "Hello, Mr. Clary," he greeted him pleasantly, "I'm Reverend Watts. Before we go in, I just want you to know that I love you and Jesus loves you."

The on-air debate ended when Watts quoted some Scripture and then asked Clary about his personal beliefs. The young Klansman broke off the debate saying, "I'm not listening to any more." He walked off the set.

As he was leaving the building, Clary and Watts met again. Clary almost pushed him out of the way, but then he saw Watts had a baby in his arms. "This is my daughter Tia," Watts said. "You say that you hate all black people. Tell me how you can hate this baby."

Clary took another look at the adorable baby and then brushed by. As he left, he heard the black minister say, "I'm going to love you and pray for you, Mr. Clary, whether you like it or not."

In the next ten years, Clary tried to make Watts hate him—and stop praying for him. Klansmen harassed the minister with phone calls, broke windows, and burned effigies on his lawn. They burned down his church and threatened his children. Finally the highway patrol had to escort the Watts children to school. But Reverend Watts continued praying.

Meanwhile Clary was moving up in Klandom and eventually was named Imperial Wizard. Yet his private life was crumbling. His wife divorced him, and he lost custody of his baby girl.

Then as he tried to unite all the hate groups—the skinheads, the neo-Nazis, the Klan, and others—he was overwhelmed by the hate. He couldn't understand it, but he was sickened by the

> There is nothing that makes us love a man so much as praying for him; and when you can once do this sincerely, you have fitted your soul for the performance of everything that is kind and civil towards him.
>
> William Law

> Prayer is the greatest force we can wield. What right have we to leave unappropriated or unapplied the greatest force which God has ordained for the salvation and transformation of men?
>
> John R. Mott

poison. He resigned his position in the Klan, went to his shabby apartment, and put a loaded gun to his head. He would end it all.

But on his bookshelf, he saw an old Bible, which reminded him of the one Reverend Watts had carried years before. He opened it to the parable of the prodigal son and read it three times before falling on his knees.

Without letting anyone know who he was, Clary joined a multiracial church, and then two years later, he decided to phone Wade Watts.

"Reverend Watts?"

The black preacher recognized the voice immediately. "Hello, Johnny Lee."

Then Clary told him what had happened. "Two years ago, I gave my heart to Jesus."

"Praise the Lord!" Watts almost shouted into the phone. "I've never stopped praying for you."

Before the conversation was over, Watts had invited Clary to speak at his church. Clary did so, telling how God had changed his heart from hate to love. At the end of the service, a teenage girl ran down the aisle to the altar. Clary saw Watts weeping. "Don't you know who that is, Johnny Lee? That's Tia. That's my baby."

What Happens When Mothers Pray

Prodigy, professor, playboy, politician—and the most influential Christian since the apostle Paul. Few names in Christianity's two-thousand-year history shine brighter than that of Augustine. Both Catholics and Protestants revere him. In the Roman church, the Augustinian order takes its name from him. Among the Protestant reformers, both Luther and Calvin regarded his writings second only to the Bible.

Yet one may wonder where Augustine would have ended up had it not been for the prayers of his mother, Monica.

Born in A.D. 354 in the little town of Tagaste, North Africa, Augustine was sent to Carthage to complete his education. In Carthage, he was recognized as a young man of genius and of strong passions. The latter led him into sensual excesses and a promiscuous lifestyle. His intellectual pride carried him into the heresy of the Manicheans and later into academic skepticism. Augustine lived with a woman he never married, and they had a child together.

His mother, a devoted Christian, was heartbroken.

When Augustine skipped town and headed for Rome, it must have seemed that Monica's prayers for her son would never be answered. Rome in the fourth century was known for its paganism and eroticism. It was the last place Monica wanted her son to go—but she didn't give up hope. In his classic autobiography, *Confessions,* Augustine recalled, "My mother, weeping . . . for me, more than mothers weep the bodily deaths of their children. And You heard her, O Lord; You heard her."

Augustine went on to write: "Almost nine years passed, in which I wallowed in the mire of that deep pit and the darkness of falsehood, often trying to rise, but dashed down the more grievously. All that time, that chaste, godly and sober widow . . . did not stop pleading for me."

His mother asked a bishop to argue with her son, but the bishop saw that Augustine was too opinionated to be won in that way. So he said to Monica, "Let him alone awhile, only pray God for him. He will of himself, by reading, find out what that error is, and how great its impiety."

In Rome Augustine taught rhetoric, but soon he moved to Milan to take a better position. There he became a personal friend of Ambrose, bishop of Milan. Influenced by Ambrose's preaching and the reading of Scripture, he was finally converted. He wrote later that when he told his mother the news, "she leaped for joy and triumph, and blessed You, who are able to do more than we ask or think." On Easter Sunday, A.D. 387, in the great Milan Cathedral, Augustine was baptized by Ambrose as Monica watched with tears rolling down her cheeks.

"It was owing to the faithful and daily prayers of my mother that I did not perish," Augustine noted.

We met many Russian "babushkas." The praying grandmothers, they were called. These were the stalwart saints of whom Stalin had cruelly said, "If we can get rid of these old women, we will have the youth in our grasp." Stalin failed. And thank God for praying grandmothers who served as a link, spanning a generation lost to atheism and connecting a new generation of young people who are asking open, honest questions about Jesus.

Joni Eareckson Tada

Later, as Augustine was accompanying his mother back to North Africa, she became ill. She told him, "Son, for my own part I have no further delight in anything in this life. . . . My hopes in this life are accomplished. One thing there was, for which I desired to linger in this life, that I might see you become a Christian before I died. My God has done this abundantly for me, that I should now see you become his servant."

Augustine went on to become the church's leading theologian, defender of the faith, preacher, and writer. Christians have much to thank Augustine for. Perhaps we should thank Monica even more.

The Prayers of "Little Bilney"

He was no Martin Luther or John Calvin, not an eloquent preacher or a forceful leader, but "Little Bilney" is famous for the fact that he cared enough to pray for someone else.

Here's the story.

Early in the sixteenth century, Thomas Bilney, a scholar at Cambridge University, was dissatisfied with life. "My soul was sick," he wrote later, "and I longed for peace, but nowhere could I find it. . . . At last I heard of Jesus." He spent what little money he had to buy a Latin translation of the New Testament. He admitted later, "I bought the book, being drawn to it rather by the Latin than by the Word of God, for at that time I did not know what the Word of God meant." And then, he says, "The light came."

On the first reading of it, as I well remember, I chanced upon these words, "This is a faithful saying, and worthy of all acceptation, that Christ Jesus came into the world to save sinners, of whom I am chief." That one sentence, through God's inward working, so lifted up my poor bruised spirit that the very bones within me leaped for joy and gladness. It was as if, after a long, dark night, day had suddenly broken.

Bilney was converted.

The most famous preacher of the day was Hugh Latimer, brilliant and eloquent, as well as a staunch foe of the Protestant Reformation. As unlikely as it appeared to be, Little Bilney wanted to see Latimer converted as he himself had been. So he prayed, "Oh God, I am but 'Little Bilney,' and shall never do any great thing for you; but give me the soul of that man, Hugh Latimer, and what wonders he shall do in your most holy name."

Then one day as Latimer was coming down from the pulpit after a sermon, he passed by Thomas Bilney, and Bilney stopped him. "Father Latimer," he whispered, "would you hear my confession?"

Latimer pointed to a side chapel, and in that side chapel Little Bilney told how he had purchased the Latin New Testament and had found the text that had changed his life. Bilney was on his knees now as he shared his story. Finally he pulled the Latin New Testament from his pocket and showed Latimer his favorite verse. "I bore the load of my sins," he said, "until . . . I saw that 'Christ Jesus came into the world to save sinners, of whom I am chief'" (1 Tim. 1:15 KJV).

Latimer was moved by Bilney's earnestness but even more by the verse of Scripture, and he experienced an instantaneous rebirth experience.

Thomas Bilney continued to speak out for what he believed, but he was arrested during the reign of Henry VIII and burned at the stake in 1531.

Latimer, on the other hand, was able to have a longer ministry, even though his fearless preaching caused him to struggle with the vicissitudes of the sixteenth-century English monarchy. He was named a bishop under Henry VIII and then imprisoned by the same king in the Tower of London. Granted a reprieve by Edward VI, he became court preacher, but when Queen Mary came to the throne, he was arrested and burned at the stake. As the fires were ablaze around him, Latimer spoke his last words: "We shall this day light such a candle by God's grace in England as I trust shall never be put out."

If you hear people say that Henry VIII started the Protestant Reformation in England, tell them that you think it may have been the prayers of Little Bilney instead.

The Depression of Mordecai Ham

For more than thirty years, Mordecai Ham had been traversing the South, preaching fiery, no-nonsense evangelistic messages in city after city. Some three hundred thousand people had professed faith in Christ and joined the church as a result of his ministry. A strong fundamentalist, he also preached against communism, evolution, and the liquor trade.

While some people disagreed with his preaching, no one could fault his personal conduct or his business practice.

Whenever Ham invaded the state of North Carolina, however, he was attacked by an agnostic newspaper editor named W. O. Saunders, who called the evangelist "an insolent mountebank, a ruthless demagogue, a preacher of hate, a joy-killer, a tyrant playing on the fears, the prejudices, and the weaknesses of unthoughtful humans." In his paper, *The Independent*, Saunders charged Ham with ruining business in every city he preached in, adding that his preaching "produces a lot of smug, bigoted, conceited, sanctimonious pigheads and pismires who think that a little blood of a lamb that they never saw has washed them whiter than snow."

Evangelist Ham kept a prayer diary, and whenever he was in North Carolina, the prayer entries frequently referred to W. O. Saunders: "And Lord, remove Saunders' influence." "Father, whatever Saunders is planning, may it be only a blunder."

126

"About Saunders, Lord, convict and save that man."

In 1934 the evangelist held his first campaign in Charlotte, North Carolina, the state's largest city. He had preached in sixteen other towns in the state, but never in Charlotte. Saunders had done his work ahead of time, warning the newspapers, business leaders, and even clergy about Ham. As Ham's biography notes, "The Charlotte meeting was particularly difficult—the Lord had to convert newspapers and ministers, as well as lay folk."

Ham was depressed and discouraged. The newspapers had condemned him and his ministry. Even pastors were speaking against him. It seemed to be the strongest opposition he had ever faced. Alone in his hotel room, he wrote out a prayer on hotel stationery:

> Dear Father, Thou knowest the conduct of all in this town: how the antichrist has made his power felt; how the ministers have opposed. . . . Deal with the newspapers. O Lord, you know how the testimony for Jesus has been opposed in this city. Deal with the city councilmen and all that would try to drive us out of the city. . . . Lord, give us a Pentecost here and deal a blow to that infidel Saunders. O Lord, please come to the help of Thy servant. Dear Father, make this the greatest meeting we have ever witnessed. . . . O Lord, I need Your endorsement. . . . In His Name. . . . M. F. Ham.

Did the Lord answer his prayer? Yes, in an unexpected way.

One evening as the evangelist gave his gospel invitation in the large temporary tabernacle on Pecan Avenue, a blond sixteen-year-old boy came forward and knelt, asking God for salvation.

Evangelist Ham, who asked God to make this "the greatest meeting we have ever witnessed," and who begged for God's "endorsement," got his prayer answered even though he didn't know it at the time. He had no idea that the teenager would become the greatest evangelist of the twentieth century. The boy's name was Billy Graham.

Between God and the devil stands the praying man.

J. Oswald Sanders

127

The Detective Had No Clothes

Charles Smedley had never really liked Christians. He had been a sailor, mortician, cook, plumber, chauffeur, and police guard in his life, and currently he was working as a detective for the Pinkerton organization, so he knew how to order people around. If Christians came knocking at his door, trying to evangelize him, he had no problem chasing them away.

That's why his family was shocked when he let his daughter's Sunday school teacher in.

For Ruth Tulley, Sunday school teaching went beyond Sundays. She wanted to meet the families of the children she taught. So when nine-year-old Laura Smedley visited her class one Sunday in 1950, Ruth Tulley decided to visit her home. All the Smedleys were surprised that Mr. Smedley invited her in to talk. The parents and the four children listened as she told them of her faith in Christ.

When Mrs. Tulley finished, she invited the family to church. Smedley laughed. "I don't have a suit of clothes to wear to church," he responded, thinking that would end the visit.

But the Sunday school teacher called his bluff. "You would come if you had a suit?"

He was still laughing when he said, "Sure." He knew he wouldn't be buying a suit anytime soon.

"Well, then," said the Sunday school teacher, "I'm just going to ask the Lord to send you a suit."

"Okay, it's a deal." With that, Mr. Smedley finally got Ruth Tulley out the door.

She went home and began praying. Meanwhile, Mr. Smedley had other problems. He didn't have a suit because he was deeply in debt. He was in debt because he couldn't hold a job. He kept losing jobs because he drank too much. Both he and his wife spent their time in French Quarter bars. They went on drinking sprees and sent their children to the movies. The state of his wardrobe was the least of his worries.

But the day after Mrs. Tulley's visit, an unexpected check came in the mail. Smedley's first thought was to celebrate at the local bars, but his wife stopped him. "Didn't we promise Mrs. Tulley that if some miracle happened and you got money for a suit, that you would go to church?"

Reluctantly Charles Smedley agreed, bought a new suit, and then accompanied his family to church. When the pastor asked if any in the congregation felt they needed prayer, Mr. Smedley raised his hand. And then the following Sunday, when the pastor gave a gospel invitation, nine-year-old Laura Smedley walked forward, and soon Charles Smedley got up out of his seat and walked forward too.

The Smedley home was completely changed, and not only the home. Smedley began talking about his faith to his old drinking buddies. Soon there were more conversions. Relatives, amazed at the change in the Smedley family, surrendered their lives to Jesus Christ too. The oldest daughter, Marty, began witnessing for Christ in high school, and she led three of her girlfriends to Christ.

Well-known Christian author James Hefley wrote this story in *Living Miracles*. He knew the story well, because Marty Smedley became his wife and a partner in his writing ministry.

One Sunday school teacher prayed for a needy family. As a result, that family was transformed. And, they figured out, the conversion of that family led to the salvation of seventy others over the next twelve years.

He Kept on Praying for Fifty-Two Years

For more than half a century, George Müller prayed for the salvation of a small group of men. Fifty-two years he prayed, and still some of them hadn't become Christians. Müller, of course, was famous for the orphanages he started, relying on faith alone. He asked God to send him the finances to care for the children, and God did. Often the answers to his prayers came just in the nick of time. (See pages 87–88.) But his prayers for the salvation of these men weren't turning out the same way— at least not for some of the men.

Müller kept careful records of everything, including his prayer requests. His prayer notebook had two-page entries, one page for requests and the opposite page for God's answers. He dated every entry, so no one would question that God had answered. Müller calculated that during his lifetime fifty thousand of his requests were answered.

Then there were these five men.

Here's how he tells it:

In November 1844, I began to pray for the conversion of five individuals. I prayed every day without a single intermission, whether sick or in health, on the land or on the seas, and whatever the pressure of my engagements might be.

Eighteen months elapsed before the first of the five was converted. I thanked God and prayed on for the others. Five years elapsed, and then the second was converted. I thanked God for the second, and prayed on for the other three. Day by day I continued to pray for them, and six years passed before the third was converted.

I thanked God for the three, and went on praying for the other two. These two remain unconverted. The man to whom God in the riches of His grace has given tens of thousands of answers to prayer in the self-same hour or day in which they were offered has been praying day by day for nearly thirty-six years for the conversion of these individuals, and yet they remain unconverted. But I hope in God, I pray on, and look yet for the answer. They are not converted yet, *but they will be.*

He wrote that after he had been praying for thirty-six years. He continued to pray until his death in 1898, more than fifty-two years in all. The two men still were not converted when Müller died. However, two years later, both of these men trusted Christ as their Savior. Müller's prayers were finally answered.

Müller never had the chance to write those men's names on the answer side of his prayer notebook. But you can be sure that God had written their names in his Book of Life.

The Miracle That Didn't Happen

"Evil spirit stick her here and there," the woman said, pointing at her little girl's stomach and then to her right ear.

Missionary Frank Ebel and his wife, Isabel, worked out of a hut (which he called his clinic) near the muddy Mucajai River in Brazil. They had been missionaries for only eight months, working with the primitive Shirishana tribe. Frank was a teacher and translator, not a doctor, but in this primitive culture, he and Isabel had to use all the medical know-how they had.

Now this mother had come to the hut, dragging a sick child behind her.

After determining that little Modit was suffering from mastoiditis and stomach cramps, Frank and Isabel administered medications to make the child as comfortable as possible. For a week they followed little Modit's progress, and they prayed fervently for her recovery, but Modit did not improve.

Finally the mother said, "Your medicine too slow," and she took her daughter across the river in a canoe to participate in a tribal festival and to see the witch doctor.

A week later, the mother returned to the Ebels' hut clinic. The missionaries saw cuts on the girl's head, arm, and legs. The witch doctor had apparently been trying to release what he thought was an evil spirit.

Frank gave the girl some penicillin and returned to his hut. A few minutes later, he heard someone cry, "Modit dead, Modit dead." Frank Ebel dashed back and applied mouth-to-mouth resuscitation, but nothing helped.

The mother pointed her finger at the missionaries, "You made Modit die." Soon a group of relatives came and took the girl's body with them.

Back in their own hut, the missionaries fell to their knees. "Lord, we don't understand why you took little Modit. But we are praying that you will yet use her death for your glory."

That afternoon the missionaries heard that the chief was coming down the jungle path with a band of men to see them.

The Ebels knew that a group of Indians had savagely beaten to death a missionary and his daughter in another part of the Brazilian jungle. Why would the chief be coming to see them now?

The chief and his men came to the porch of the Ebels' hut and sat down. Frank and Isabel said nothing, waiting for the chief to break the silence. Finally the chief spoke.

"You go away?"

"No," Frank responded, "we don't want to. We love you. Do you want us to go?"

Another pause. Then the chief continued, "We want you to stay. You are good. You tell us more about a good God." Then the chief rose and walked away, leading his entourage up the jungle trail.

The Ebels looked at each other in amazement. Once the Indian party had disappeared into the jungle, Isabel asked, "Remember our prayer?"

Frank nodded. "I asked God to use little Modit's death for his glory."

It was a turning point. Not long afterward, the chief's son professed faith in Christ, and five other tribesmen followed. Then the chief ordered the entire village to move across the river to be closer to the missionaries.

God works in odd ways. You would think that only a miraculous healing would persuade a tribe of God's power. But somehow the passing of this sick child—and the missionaries' loving attention to her—was even more powerful.

He Had Heard It All Before

Jack Luckey had heard it all before. Raised in a godly home in the shadow of a Christian college, he knew all the answers. By the time he was a teenager, he had heard hundreds of sermons and altar calls; he was no longer touched by even the most fervent appeals. And then he rebelled, trying to forget all about God. He didn't need any of that stuff—prayer, faith, the Bible—

the whole Christianity bit. Sunday school naïveté was gone forever. The whole concept of God now seemed irrational to him;
Christianity just didn't make sense.

Jack married Camilla, a college friend who had also been
raised in the church but had drifted far from it. Eight years
later, however, she started going to church, reading her Bible,
and praying for her husband. His strident atheism was being
tested. For almost two years, she prayed for him, but he seemed
as resistant as ever. As a dutiful husband, he went occasionally
to her Episcopal church. These services were different from the
camp meetings and altar calls with which he had grown up, so
he felt he could safely guard his rebellion. When his wife walked
forward to take communion, he would often walk up with her,
but before reaching the communion rail, he would turn left and
slip out a side door to light up a cigarette.

"If there really is a God, he would . . . ," Jack began saying
more and more. He thought he was confirming his atheism by
noting all the occasions when God could act but didn't. Yet that
possibility actually began opening him up to the idea of an
active God. In a way, it was a challenge . . . and God took it.

One Saturday in 1982, Camilla lost her Bible, and Jack helped
her look for it. They scoured the house—no Bible. He went into
the backyard, saying, "If there really is a God and if he really
cares for Camilla, he would show us where that [blankety-
blank] Bible is." And just then he kicked a bucket in the backyard, and out flew the Bible. What would her Bible be doing in
a bucket in the backyard?

The next day he went to church with her. "The Bible in the
bucket" was still in Jack's mind. When parishioners were invited
forward to take communion, he got up as usual to go with
Camilla. But this time he was torn. Should he walk out the side
door for a smoke as he always did, or should he stay and take
communion? For some reason, an old hymn came into his
mind. It was sung in his home church when people walked forward—"Just As I Am." The folks in this Episcopal church had
probably never heard that song, he figured. "If there really is a
God," Jack said to himself, "they should sing 'Just As I Am.' If
that unlikely thing happens, then I will take communion."

Moments later, the church musicians started playing those familiar strains: "Just as I am, without one plea."

As Jack walked forward, he felt he heard God saying to him, "Jack, you know I'm here. Now what are you going to do about it? You can turn left and leave by the side door and I will leave you alone, or you can turn right to the communion rail and come to me."

Jack made a right turn.

The very next day, Jack had his third "if God" epiphany. He rode his bike each day between his job in Washington, D.C., and his home in Alexandria, Virginia. But daylight saving time had just expired, and now it was dark for his ride home. He turned on his bicycle light; nothing happened. It would be dangerous to ride all that way with heavy automobile traffic around him, but what could he do? He could pray.

It was another "if" prayer. "God, if you really love me, you'd give me light." Reaching forward, he flicked on the bicycle light, and it glowed brightly. He rode all the way home with light, and as soon as he reached home, the light went out again. The light got its power from a generator—but then Jack remembered removing some parts from the generator months earlier. He had intended to replace them but never had. Checking the generator, he saw these parts were still missing. There was no way this bicycle light should have worked, but somehow God had supplied power for his ride home.

Jack Luckey still recalls the weekend with his three "if" prayers: "Here was the God of the universe, who took the time to show me he was there, when I was such a stubborn jerk."

10

People You May Know

Famous People Relying on Prayer

Now when Daniel learned that the decree had been published, he went home to his upstairs room where the windows opened toward Jerusalem. Three times a day he got down on his knees and prayed, giving thanks to his God, just as he had done before.

Daniel 6:10

A candy maker, a young widow, a brilliant atheist, a White House lawyer. What do they have in common? They turned to God in prayer. And God used them to influence millions.

We must always be careful when talking about "famous Christians." Our world has made fame an idol. We often assume that famous people are better than we are, or at least more blessed. In a book like this, we're tempted to say, "Hey, these folks were nobodies, and then they prayed, and God answered by making them famous!"

But that's not the point.

The New Testament writer James referred to an Old Testament celebrity, Elijah, to teach about prayer. Elijah, he wrote,

135

was just like us. He shared our human passions. There was nothing all that special about him. But he prayed and things happened. Without question, God's power worked miracles, not Elijah's.

And so it is with our hall of fame in these pages. Billy Graham, Bill Bright, and Francis Schaeffer each faced crippling doubts about his calling and his faith, but he prayed and God answered. Mother Teresa gave away her last rupee; Catherine Marshall faced a terrifying disease. They prayed and God showed his power. We admire these people, but we don't worship them. The truth is that you have access to that same power, whether or not you're famous now or ever will be. If you're doubting, if you're struggling to make ends meet, if you can't get out of bed in the morning, talk to God about it. He's ready to show his power in you and through you.

> *Give me, O Lord, a steadfast heart,*
> *which no unworthy affection may drag downwards;*
> *give me an unconquered heart,*
> *which no tribulation can wear out;*
> *give me an upright heart,*
> *which no unworthy purpose may tempt aside.*
>
> Thomas Aquinas

Brother Andrew's Prayer

Lord, Make Seeing Eyes Blind

A skilled smuggler, he secretly ferried thousands of contraband materials across national boundaries. He crossed the Iron Curtain again and again, sneaking illegal objects past the border patrols. What was his dangerous cargo? Bibles.

In his best-selling book, *God's Smuggler,* Brother Andrew told of the miracles and answers to prayer that accompanied his dangerous missions as he tried to carry God's Word to citizens of an atheistic regime.

Raised in a small town in the Netherlands, Brother Andrew fought with Dutch forces in Indonesia when he was only seventeen. The cruelty of the war numbed him into spiritual apathy, but in a veterans' hospital, God got hold of him.

He went to a Bible school in England; later he was invited by the Communists to a youth rally in Poland. When he saw the spiritual hunger of the people in Eastern Europe, he resolved to do something about it. He had noticed an odd occurrence in the Polish church services he attended. The minister would announce his Bible text, and then the people would cluster closely around the few in the congregation who had Bibles. The point was clear: They needed more Bibles.

In 1957 Brother Andrew, still in his twenties, received a visa to enter another Communist country, Yugoslavia. After scouring Amsterdam for any kind of Christian printed material in Slavic languages, he headed toward the Yugoslav border. "For the first time in my life," he says, "I was about to enter a Communist country on my own." Previously, he had always traveled with a group.

He knew the risks. The Yugoslav government had recently decreed that visitors could bring in only articles for their personal use. Anything that was brought in new or in quantity was suspect. Material that had been printed outside the country was regarded as foreign propaganda. Brother Andrew was driving a new VW that was "literally bulging with tracts, Bibles, and portions of Bibles." How could he get them across the border?

He stopped and prayed, and his prayer was one that he repeated over and over again in coming years. It was simply this: "Lord, in my luggage I have Scripture that I want to take to your children across this border. When you were on earth, you made blind eyes see. Now, I pray, make seeing eyes blind. Do not let the guards see those things you do not want them to see."

So with this prayer in his heart, he started his car and approached the checkpoint. The two guards seemed pleased to

> My prayers seem to be more of an attitude than anything else. I indulge in no lip service, but ask the great God silently, daily and often many times a day, to permit me to speak to Him. I ask Him to give me wisdom, understanding and bodily strength to do His will. Hence, I am asking and receiving all the time.
>
> George Washington Carver

meet someone from the Netherlands, and Brother Andrew chatted with them in German. They poked around in his camping gear, and then asked him to open a suitcase. When the guard lifted the shirts, a pile of Christian tracts was clearly visible.

"Anything to declare?" asked one of the guards.

"Only some small things," replied Brother Andrew. Yes, the tracts were quite small.

"We won't bother with them," said the guard. Andrew closed the suitcase, was handed his passport, and went on his way to Zagreb.

Later in Belgrade, when he urged a congregation to pray and read their Bibles, the people did not respond. "Prayer, yes," the pastor explained. "That we can do each day. But Bible reading. Few of these people have Bibles."

That night Brother Andrew said, "A resolve was born in me. . . . I promised God that as often as I could lay my hands on a Bible, I would bring it to these children of his behind the wall that men had built."

Time after time, Brother Andrew crossed the border into Eastern European countries, and time after time God blinded the eyes of the guards as Andrew brought Bibles to Christians who desperately needed them.

Bill Bright's Prayer

Confirm the Vision, Lord

Bill Bright never stopped coming up with revolutionary ideas. As the founder of Campus Crusade for Christ, he revolutionized campus evangelism. Today, Campus Crusade is one of the largest faith mission organizations in the world, doing much more than simply reaching college kids. One of Bright's bright ideas was to condense the gospel message into four basic points. Now known as the *Four Spiritual Laws,* this may be the most widely used evangelistic tract in the world. And then came the film *Jesus,* which Campus Crusade brought to the world. More than three hundred organizations are using the film, and an estimated 10 percent of the world has seen it.

> What I have considered lofty spirituality is sham and humbug in Your eyes. Worse than that, often it has been a cloak to hide my fear of not receiving what I ask You for.
>
> Catherine Marshall

But Bill Bright might have gone back to making candy if God had not spectacularly answered one prayer in 1951.

He had been doing quite well with Bright's Confections and Bright's Brandied Food. Business was booming, major American department stores were clamoring for his products, and he was starting to export overseas. He was, he admits, "a happy pagan."

Then, shortly after his conversion, Bill Bright entered seminary, and one night while studying for a Hebrew exam, he had an indescribable vision. "All I can say is that I met God. . . . I have never been the same since." He says that he was specifically called to "reach the campus for Christ today—reach the world for Christ tomorrow."

So despite his wife's misgivings, he quit seminary and began preparing for campus ministry, drafting a plan and asking Christian leaders to serve on his board. Yet one troubling fact remained. Although he had spoken at gatherings of students, he had yet to see any student converted as a result of his ministry.

Was he all wrong about the vision? Did God really want him in student evangelism? He had gone to college in Oklahoma, and now he was in Los Angeles—was there a different kind of student here, more resistant to the Christian message? In any case, how could he be involved in campus evangelism if students weren't being won to Christ through his ministry?

Bill and his wife, Vonette, gathered some students together at the Kappa Alpha Theta sorority house at UCLA. Beforehand, Bright was nervous. "O Lord," he prayed, "please let there be at least one who will respond, to confirm the vision you gave me."

Then he spoke to the students about Jesus and how they could know him personally. He closed by asking anyone who wanted to receive Christ as Lord and Savior to come and talk to him afterward. When he finished with a closing prayer, a line started forming in front of him. Sixty women were present in the meeting, and more than half were standing in the line wanting to know how to receive Christ. In the next few months, more than 250 UCLA students became Christians at similar meetings, including the student body president, the student newspaper editor, and several of the school's top athletes.

Bill Bright's prayer was dramatically answered, the vision was confirmed, and Campus Crusade was launched.

Today, Campus Crusade is operating more than sixty different ministries with a full-time staff of seventeen thousand and a trained volunteer staff of more than two hundred thousand. The total distribution of the *Four Spiritual Laws* tract has now exceeded 2.5 billion copies, and the cumulative audience for the *Jesus* film has exceeded 450 million people. How many have come to know Christ through Bright's ministry? Maybe millions.

But fifty years ago, he had prayed for at least one.

Mother Teresa's Prayer

Only You

There she stood, all alone on the streets of Calcutta's slums—no shelter, no company, no helper, no money, no employment, no promise, no guarantee, no security.

This little Albanian woman, born Agnes Gonxha Bojaxhiu, had been a nun teaching at the Loreto convent in Calcutta for almost two decades. But now she had left the comfortable convent because she felt God was calling her to serve "the poorest of the poor." In Loreto she says she "was the happiest nun in the world." It meant everything to her. To leave it was the "most difficult thing I have ever done. It was much more difficult than to leave my family and country to enter religious life."

At Loreto she had material security. She never had to search for food, medicine, or clothing, and never had a concern about safety. But now she was out on the streets of Calcutta—alone.

> When thou prayest, rather let thy heart be without words than thy words without heart. Prayer will make a man cease from sin, or sin will entice a man to cease from prayer.
>
> John Bunyan

Loreto had been blocked off from the slums by high walls. On the grounds were lovely, peaceful gardens, and the yellow-washed walls were cheerful and pleasant. The girls she taught were daughters of Calcutta's wealthier families. Returning from weekends in which they visited hospitals, students told of the abject poverty and disease in the streets, and Mother Teresa had seen it too—the leprosy victims begging, the little children starving, the bundles of rags on the sidewalks that turned out to be people.

Once, after writing her own mother about the pleasantness of the Loreto convent, she received a reply: "My dearest daughter, do not forget that you went out there to help the poor."

Then on a train trip into the Himalayan foothills, as she was quietly praying, she received what she referred to as "her call within a call." "The message was quite clear," she said later. "I was to leave the convent and help the poor while living among them. It was an order."

It was one thing to get an order from God and another thing to get official permission to leave the convent. But eventually it came, and then the door of the convent closed behind her and Mother Teresa was on her own.

> When we come to the end of ourselves, we come to the beginning of God.
>
> Billy Graham

Well, not entirely on her own. Alone in Calcutta's slums, she prayed, "My God, you, only you. I trust in your call, your inspiration. You will not let me down."

With faith that God would not let her down, she said, "I was sure that the Lord wanted me to be where I was."

On her first day along Calcutta's streets, a priest came up to her and begged for a contribution. She had five rupees when she started her walk, but she had given four of them to the poor. She hesitated at first to give the remaining rupee to the priest, but then she did, and so she had absolutely nothing left.

But that afternoon the same priest found her and gave her an envelope. A man had given him the envelope to give to Mother Teresa, the priest explained. The man had heard about what she wanted to do and wanted to help her. When she looked in the envelope, she found fifty rupees.

Mother Teresa started by finding a clearing in the garbage of a public park and gathering a small group of children to teach them the alphabet. She visited in their homes, bringing them what food and medical help she could. Sometimes she begged when necessary and then gave away everything she had.

One night she heard a knock on her door. A frail-looking girl was there, saying, "Mother, I have come to join you."

Mother Teresa turned to the Lord and thanked him, "Dear Jesus, how good you are. You keep the promise you made me. Lord Jesus, thank you for your goodness." The girl became the first of Mother Teresa's Missionaries of Charity. There would be many more.

In 1979, after decades of service to India's poor, Mother Teresa was awarded the Nobel Peace Prize.

What God accomplished through her was an amazing answer to her simple prayer, "My God, you, only you. I trust in your call, your inspiration. You will never let me down."

Billy Graham's Prayer

Oh God, Use Me a Little Bit

Altoona was a flop. Doubts were swirling around him. In 1949 evangelist Billy Graham wasn't sure what to do next.

If he couldn't succeed as an evangelist in Altoona, Pennsylvania, why bother? He thought about quitting the evangelism business altogether. At the age of thirty, he was already serving as president of a small Christian college without an advanced degree. Maybe he should go back to school for a Ph.D.

But the biggest problem he had was his questions. "My very faith was under siege," he recalled later.

His close friend Charles Templeton, with whom he had conducted evangelistic campaigns, was having second thoughts about the authority of Scripture, and as Graham was reading the writings of various theologians, he began to have some questions too. He never doubted the core of the gospel message or the deity of Christ, but he wondered if the Bible could be trusted completely. So many apparent contradictions existed for which he had no answer; how could he go on doing what he had been doing?

The conservative school he led was committed to the full inspiration and total inerrancy of Scripture. How could he continue to serve as its president? And how could he as an evangelist say, "The Bible says . . . ," when he had such doubts? He felt like a hypocrite.

He began studying everything the Bible had to say about itself and read everything he could find on every side of the issue. He looked at what Jesus had to say about Scripture. One evening he looked at every verse of Scripture that used the phrase, "Thus saith the Lord."

At a July conference in Michigan, still wracked with doubt, he prayed with two other ministers, saying, "Oh, if somehow the Lord could use me a little bit."

A big evangelistic campaign was coming up in Los Angeles. Graham wondered how he could preach with so many questions. Maybe he should pull out of it, cancel it.

> The confession of evil works is the first beginning of good works.
>
> Augustine

Then at a conference in California, Graham took an evening walk in the San Bernardino Mountains. When he saw a tree stump in the woods, he fell to his knees in front of it. He opened his Bible on the stump, even though it was too dark to read anything in the dim moonlight.

And there he prayed. As he recalled in his autobiography, *Just As I Am*, the prayer went something like this: "O God! There are many things in this book I do not understand. There are many problems with it for which I have no solution. . . . I can't answer some of the philosophical and psychological questions about it. . . . But Father, I am going to accept this as Thy Word—by faith."

When he arose from his knees, he says that he "sensed the presence and power of God as I had not sensed it in months. . . . A major bridge had been crossed. . . . A spiritual battle had been fought and won."

It looked for a while that fall as if the Los Angeles crusade would be a bigger flop than Altoona, but then, surprisingly, newspapers started giving it headlines, and *Time* magazine did a major story. Within a year, *Newsweek* was calling Graham "America's greatest living evangelist."

Now when Billy Graham announced, "The Bible says . . . ," he was speaking from his heart. His nighttime prayer of abandonment to the Word of God brought new power and authority to his message. His unashamed faithfulness to Scripture, coupled with his totally sincere belief in its truth, has been perhaps the major factor under God in his success as an evangelist.

Indeed, God has used him "a little bit."

Francis Schaeffer's Prayer

Father, Show Us What to Do

They felt they were living in a fog. The Schaeffers were rocked by several tragedies between 1950 and 1955 and weren't sure how to cope. "We didn't know what we were doing," Edith Schaeffer wrote later in *The Tapestry.*

In those years, Edith had a miscarriage; an infant son contracted polio, and a daughter became seriously ill. The Schaeffers served as missionaries in Switzerland, but a split occurred in the denomination that sponsored them. Churches were told to stop sending them money. Longtime friends turned their backs on them.

> As it is the business of tailors to make clothes and cobblers to mend shoes, so it is the business of Christians to pray.
>
> Martin Luther

Along with these trials, and probably because of them, Francis Schaeffer was wrestling with a crisis of faith. What on earth were they doing in mission work? How could they do any kind of ministry?

Yet in those difficult years, the Schaeffers learned much about prayer. "Prayer," wrote Edith, "is not a push button in some sort of vending machine that connects the earth with the throne of the living God. . . . We are not promised freedom from hardship on the basis of prayer. We are promised answers, including comfort in sorrow, sufficient grace to bear the 'thorn in the flesh,' and also answers which supply our needs in a variety of ways, at very different times of life."

While on furlough in the States, the Schaeffers discovered the serious problems their mission board and denomination were having. Would they remain missionaries without financial support? Already they had made tentative reservations on a ship going back to Europe. Should they cancel those reservations? While Francis was on a speaking tour, Edith and the children prayed about their situation. If God wanted them to go back to Europe, they asked, would he send them the money by July 29? The children posted a drawing of a big thermometer on the dining room wall. As gifts arrived, they took a red pencil to the thermometer to make the temperature rise. And when the red in the thermometer went over the top, Edith wrote, "there was jumping and squealing."

On shipboard, they explained why they were going back to Europe despite all the problems. "We were coming back to live

The dear God hears
and pities all;
He knoweth all our
wants;
And what we
blindly ask of him
His love withholds
or grants.

And so I sometimes
think our prayers
Might well be
merged in one,
And nest and perch
and hearth and
church
Repeat, "Thy will be
done."

John Greenleaf
Whittier

with more reality on the basis of prayer, asking that the Lord would give us his strength moment by moment." On the ocean liner, Francis mentioned that a good name for their chalet in Switzerland might be *L'Abri*, which means "shelter" in French. Soon both Francis and Edith were talking about making their home a spiritual shelter where young people could come for coffee, tea, and answers to their questions.

Back in Switzerland, their problems continued, but the Schaeffers kept praying, "Father, show us what to do. Father, show us what to do." Each impossibility was met with a miraculous answer to prayer. Their polio-stricken son, Franky, recovered and was left with no paralysis. When they needed to find a new place for L'Abri, a new site became available at the last moment. For the down payment, gifts in varying amounts were received from 156 scattered people and totaled exactly enough. Finally, on the weekend of May 6–9, 1955, L'Abri was born.

"After that first weekend," Edith wrote, "we never had a time without someone arriving on the doorstep with questions." Soon young people from around the world were streaming to L'Abri to talk. One secular publication described Schaeffer as a "spiritual guru to young students struggling with existential and philosophical problems of the 20th century." L'Abri became a study center and a meeting place for seekers as well as thoughtful believers. Later, similar communities were developed in four other countries.

Prayer had lifted the fog. Now the Schaeffers knew exactly what God wanted them to do.

Catherine Marshall's Prayer

I Am Beaten, I Am Whipped, I Am Through

The young widow had to find a way to support herself and her young son, so she tried writing. Good choice. She became one of the most popular Christian writers of the twentieth century.

Peter Marshall, the celebrated chaplain of the United States Senate and pastor of Washington's New York Presbyterian Church, died suddenly in 1949, leaving Catherine Marshall a widow at age thirty-five. Picking up the pieces emotionally, she also picked up portions of her late husband's sermons. The sermon collection sold more than a million copies. She went on to write his biography, *A Man Called Peter,* which was made into a Hollywood movie.

Her novel *Christy* also became a best-seller and later a TV series. Catherine Marshall's nonfiction books such as *Adventures in Prayer, Meeting God at Every Turn,* and *Beyond Ourselves* established her as a thoughtful writer who approached the Christian life honestly and fervently.

Writing in *Guideposts* in 1972, she admitted, "Healing through faith remains a mystery to me. . . . As a young wife and mother, I myself was wonderfully healed. At the time of Peter Marshall's first heart attack, he was brought back from the brink of death, yet went on into the next life three years later. And despite an all-out prayer effort, the baby daughter born one summer to my son Peter John and his wife Edith lived on this earth but six weeks. Why? There are no glib answers."

Her personal healing was a turning point in her life. Stricken with tuberculosis while her husband was getting busier and busier in Washington, D.C., she prayed, demanding that God heal her. Her husband needed her, her infant son needed her, and the church needed her. It all made good sense—why couldn't God see it the way she did?

Months went by and she wasn't healed. Then one day her husband gave her a tract describing the experience of a missionary in China. The missionary's problem was similar to hers;

> My words fly up,
> my thoughts
> remain below;
> Words without
> thoughts never to
> heaven go.
>
> William
> Shakespeare

in fact, even the missionary's prayer was similar to hers.

After reading the tract, Catherine saw how shallow her faith was. She was self-centered, not really concerned for others. She lacked the love and compassion of Jesus Christ.

So finally she prayed, "Lord, I've done everything that I know how, but it hasn't been good enough. I am weary of struggling with your will, trying to get from you what I want. I am beaten, I am whipped, I am through. If you want me to be an invalid all the rest of my life and to stay right in this bed until death comes, here I am, I am ready. Do anything that you like with me and my life."

At that point God took over. In a short time, Catherine was healed, back on her feet, full of life, full of faith, and full of strength. Because of what she went through, because she had walked through the valley of the shadow of death, she was able to be an encouragement to countless others.

"His Spirit," Catherine wrote later, "sometimes confounds us, often amazes us and is always the Guide to the future who can bring us joy and exciting fulfillment."

C. S. Lewis's Prayer

He Was the Hunter, I Was the Deer

C. S. Lewis was an atheist and proud of it. A brilliant scholar, he had gotten a first-class degree from Oxford University and was now a fellow at Oxford's Magdalen College. He was still in his twenties when God started closing in on him.

"I never had the experience of looking for God," Lewis wrote later. "It was the other way round. He was the hunter (or so it seemed to me) and I was the deer. He stalked me . . . took unerring aim, and fired."

148

In general, the young Lewis didn't want to be interfered with. "I had wanted to call my soul my own." But his atheism started to collapse when some of his closest friends began to admit that they believed in God. "Early in 1926," Lewis recalls, "the hardest boiled of all the atheists I ever knew sat in my room on the other side of the fire and remarked that the evidence for the historicity of the Gospels was really surprisingly good."

> What in me is dark, Illumine, what is low, raise and support.
>
> John Milton

Lewis was stunned. If this friend, "the cynic of cynics," was succumbing to faith, what would happen to Clive Staples Lewis? "A young atheist cannot guard his faith too carefully. Dangers lie in wait for him on every side."

Two Christian writers, G. K. Chesterton and George MacDonald, were among Lewis's favorites. (He considered Chesterton "the most sensible man alive, apart from his Christianity.") Their works influenced young Lewis as the divine hunter continued to take aim at his heart.

Then as he was teaching philosophy at Oxford, Lewis struggled to find a philosophical position that satisfied him. He finally left a spot open for God, allowing that a "philosophical God or god" might exist but holding that there was "no possibility of being in a personal relation with Him."

He was being forced to make a decision. It was safe to think of God philosophically, but God wouldn't let him stay there. "Total surrender, the absolute leap in the dark, were demanded. . . .The demand was not even 'All or nothing.' . . . Now, the demand was simply 'All.'"

Then in 1929, at age thirty-one, Lewis says he "gave in, and admitted God was God, and knelt and prayed." What he said in his prayer is not known; it may have been simply, "I give in," or "You exist." But we do know he called himself "the most dejected and reluctant convert in all England. I did not then see what is now the most shining and obvious thing: the Divine humility which will accept a convert even on such terms."

How does God answer a prayer like that? No real request is made, except perhaps to start a relationship. The "reluctant convert" bows before the Almighty and says, "Do with me what you will." God responds by drawing that person into a meaningful relationship. Lewis compared his own return to that of the prodigal son, whose prepared speech ("Make me a hired hand") was cut short by his father's embrace.

This prayer was just the first step in Lewis's conversion. He had been converted to a general belief in God but not yet to biblical Christianity. He struggled with this step also, but it finally occurred, oddly enough, on a trip to the zoo. Once again, Lewis was vague on the details. "When we set out I did not believe that Jesus Christ is the Son of God and when we reached the zoo I did." At that point, his whole life was changed, and for the next three decades, he was enormously productive, penning books of fantasy, apologetics, and discipleship.

Lewis continued to teach at Oxford and Cambridge and gained an international reputation for his scholarship. But his clever writing made him one of the most influential Christians of the twentieth century. His simple prayer of faith was answered with God's mighty faithfulness.

Charles Colson's Prayer

Somehow I Want to Give Myself to You

It was 1973. The Watergate scandal was breaking, and the president's lawyer was in deep trouble. Charles Colson had been a tough guy in the Nixon administration, but now he felt the ground caving in beneath him.

He phoned a friend, Tom Phillips, president of Raytheon Corporation, and asked to meet with him. Why meet with Phillips? Colson wasn't sure, but the last time they had talked, Phillips had said, "I have accepted Jesus Christ and committed my life." Though Colson didn't know what that meant, something in Tom's demeanor had assured Colson it was very real.

When they met, Phillips asked if Colson wanted to accept Christ too; Colson declined. He knew about foxhole religion from his experience in the marines, and he didn't want to turn to God as the easy way out. And besides, "I've got a lot of intellectual hang-ups to get past," he said.

Phillips gave him a copy of C. S. Lewis's *Mere Christianity.* "Let me know what you think of that book, will you?" Phillips asked. And then Colson went out to his car.

In the darkness, Colson started to cry. He started the car's engine. Mad at himself for showing emotion, he reviled himself, "What kind of a weakness is this?" He started to drive away, but a hundred yards down the road he had to pull over to the side and sob.

And now he prayed what he called his first real prayer: "God, I don't know how to find you, but I'm going to try! I'm not much the way I am now, but somehow I want to give myself to you." And then, not knowing what to say, he simply repeated two words, "Take me, take me, take me."

He had no idea what was happening. What was he surrendering? What was this all about? Whatever it was, for the first time in his life, he felt that he was not alone anymore.

The next day, he was still trying to figure it out. He had surrendered himself to someone or something, but he wasn't quite sure what. He took out the book by C. S. Lewis and, like the lawyer that he was, put it alongside a yellow pad on which to write his notes. He wrote at the top of the pad: "Is there a God?"

After filling up sheet after sheet of his yellow pads, he found himself faced with the question that C. S. Lewis had posed: Was Jesus Christ a lunatic or was he God incarnate? There seemed to be no other options. And if Jesus Christ was indeed God, then he deserved to be the Lord of his life. There was no way around it. He had to believe or disbelieve.

At that point, Colson realized what he had done when a few days earlier he had repeated, "Take me, take me, take me." And now he said the words, "Lord Jesus, I believe you. I accept you. Please come into my life. I commit it to you."

He wrote to Tom Phillips, told him of the step he had taken, and asked for prayer. Colson would need it.

For his role in the Watergate affair, he was imprisoned for seven months, and when he was released, he faced widespread

When life knocks you to your knees, that's the best position in which to pray. That's where I learned.

Ethel Barrymore

skepticism about the reality of his conversion. But moved by compassion for prisoners, he founded Prison Fellowship Ministries, working for justice, reform, and evangelism. Since then he has written numerous best-sellers and has become one of the most trusted thinkers and spokesmen in the evangelical church. In 1993 he was awarded the Templeton Prize for Progress in Religion.

Decades later, few could deny that when Colson said, "Take me, take me, take me," he really meant it. His prayer was amazingly answered.

11

Who Needs to Be a Millionaire?

God's Provision for Those in Need

And my God will meet all your needs according to his glorious riches in Christ Jesus.

Philippians 4:19

Money. That's all you Christians ever think about.

That's a common opinion among non-Christians, and it's not entirely wrong. Well, it's not *all* we think about. We do spend time focusing on, say, the grace of God and the salvation of the world. But flip through a few TV or radio frequencies, or visit a handful of churches, or actually read through the many fundraising letters you receive from Christian ministries and you might begin to agree. We tend to talk about money a lot.

Maybe that's not all bad.

Money is a fact of life. Everyone thinks about it. People love it, want it, waste it, hoard it, and fight over it. Christians talk about money because we share it, give it, use it, and sacrifice it. Sure, there are some greedy Christians. Some even try to use prayer to build their own financial fortunes (and teach others to do this). Woe to them. As you'll see in this chapter, however, a number of Christians humbly rely on God for the daily subsistence of their own lives and of their ministries.

Money is power, some say. Well, God shows his power in our world in many ways. Sometimes he chooses to provide the money we need to do good things.

Lord, You look after my business and I will look after Yours.

John R. Rice

Saved by Two Carloads of Cattle

The school's founder had great dreams for its future, but at the time it didn't seem to have a future.

Theologian Lewis Sperry Chafer started a seminary in 1924, christening it the Evangelical Theological College. Later known as Dallas Theological Seminary, it became one of the largest seminaries in the United States, but shortly after its first class of thirteen students arrived, it was, for all practical purposes, bankrupt. Creditors were crying for their money, and the school's coffers were empty.

Lenders notified school officials that they would foreclose on a particular day at twelve noon if they weren't paid. The board of directors gathered in the president's office on that day to pray.

These men felt certain that it was God's will to launch the seminary, and they couldn't believe that God would not somehow provide for it to continue. Yet as the minutes ticked away, it seemed impossible.

In the prayer meeting was Harry Ironside, a nationally known Bible teacher who later became pastor of Chicago's Moody

Memorial Church for two decades. Ironside was known for his down-to-earth style in both preaching and praying. So when it was his turn to pray, he said in his candid way, "Lord, we know that the cattle on a thousand hills are thine. Please sell some of them and send us the money."

The others in the room might have been surprised by the tone of that prayer, but they said their amens anyway. What they didn't know was that, about that same time, a tall Texan in boots and an open-collar shirt was strolling into the business office of the seminary.

"Howdy!" he said to the secretary. "I just sold two carloads of cattle over in Fort Worth. I've been trying to make a business deal go through, but it just won't work. I feel God wants me to give this money to the seminary. I don't know if you need it or not, but here's the check."

The secretary looked twice at the check, said thank you, and then took the check to the president's office. She wasn't sure whether she should interrupt a prayer meeting of such distinguished ministers and theologians, but she knew the critical nature of the hour, so she timidly tapped at the door.

President Lewis Sperry Chafer answered. The secretary told him that she was sorry to interrupt, but a man had just come and delivered the check to her, and she wanted to bring it to Dr. Chafer as quickly as possible.

Chafer recognized the name on the check as that of a well-known cattleman in the area, so it was certainly legitimate. Then he looked more closely at the amount of the check, and he was flabbergasted. It was the exact sum of the debt that the creditors were demanding.

Turning to Ironside, he said, "Harry, God sold the cattle."

Delivery Service for Billy Bray

On his deathbed, Billy Bray asked his doctor to tell him honestly, "How is it?"

"You are going to die," the doctor answered.

155

> "If you remain in me and my words remain in you, ask whatever you wish, and it will be given you."
>
> John 15:7

Bray's response was nearly a shout: "Glory! Glory be to God! I shall soon be in heaven!"

That's the kind of guy Billy Bray was. He worked as a miner in Cornwall, England, but he was hardly a typical mine worker. When he wasn't down in the mines, he was building chapels or preaching somewhere, anywhere. Whatever he did, he was full of praise. Some people didn't think he had much to praise God for, because his family was very poor—and he didn't help matters much when he gave what he had to people who had less than he had.

It cost money for Billy Bray to build chapels, but that was an ability he wanted to give back to the Lord, and he expected that somehow the Lord would provide the necessary funds or material.

Once he had just completed a chapel at Kerley Downs, but he had no money to buy a pulpit. Then Billy saw a notice for a nearby auction of old furniture, and a three-cornered cupboard was going to be put up for sale. He was already envisioning what he could do to convert that cupboard into a pulpit.

Though Billy knew a lot about building, he knew nothing about auctions. After praying about it, he went to the auction anyway, even though he had no money in his pockets. When he got there, he asked a man near him what the cupboard would sell for. "About six shillings," the man replied and then asked, "Aren't you the chap that builds chapels?" When Billy Bray told him why he was interested in the cupboard, the man handed him six shillings as a gift for the chapel. Then the bidding began, and Billy immediately bid six shillings, thinking that he would be given the cupboard immediately. To his chagrin, a man behind him bid seven and took it.

Billy Bray was astonished. He was sure that the Lord wanted him to have that cupboard for his chapel. "But Father knows best," he said. "Anyway, I must give the man back his six shillings." He looked for the man, but he was gone, so Billy walked back to the pulpitless chapel to pray about the situation. "What did the Lord have in mind?" he wondered.

156

When he came out of the chapel after praying, his faith was renewed. The Lord must have another plan, he felt, so he looked both ways to see what the Lord would do next. Then he saw a cart coming up the hill . . . carrying the cupboard. Curiously he followed it. "They carried it to a house and tried to take it inside," he reported later, "but it was just too big to get in. They twisted and turned, they pulled and pushed, but it was no use."

The purchaser of the cupboard was disgusted. "Here's a mess," he said. "I've given seven shillings for it, and now all I can do is chop it up for firewood."

Billy Bray stepped forward and put his hand on the man's shoulder. "I'll give you six shillings for it if you will carry it down to my little chapel." The man was glad to accept Bray's offer.

"Bless the Lord!" said Billy with joy. "It's just like him. He knew I couldn't carry it myself, so he got this man to carry it for me."

The Hour of Decision for the *Hour of Decision*

Ninety-two thousand dollars sounded like a lot of money. It *was* a lot of money, especially for a country preacher just beginning to gain national fame. Billy Graham had an opportunity to do a coast-to-coast weekly radio broadcast on the ABC network. But thirteen weeks would cost ninety-two thousand dollars. How would he ever raise that money?

The year 1950 was a pivotal time in religious communications. The early pioneers of radio preaching were reaching the end of their ministries. Walter A. Maier, whose preaching on *The Lutheran Hour* reached an estimated twenty million listeners, passed away that year at the age of fifty-seven. Charles E. Fuller, speaker on the equally popular *Old Fashioned Revival Hour*, was nearing retirement age. Theodore Elsner, president of the newly formed National Religious Broadcasters, was concerned.

Who would replace these radio pioneers when they died? Television had been launched only a few years before, and no religious personalities had established themselves as yet in that new medium. Radio still had a powerful presence. What new preacher could step up and use it for God's glory?

Elsner became convinced that evangelist Billy Graham was that person. Graham had previous radio experience on a Chicago station, and now he had become nationally known from the success of his Los Angeles revival. He'd be a natural. Elsner broached the subject with Graham—and was turned down. The evangelist was already overloaded with his crusades in various cities. A radio ministry would take too many hours each week.

A month later, Elsner sent Walter Bennett and Fred Dienert, two advertising executives who specialized in buying time for religious programs, to see Graham. They told the evangelist that a choice time slot on Sunday afternoons would soon be available on the ABC radio network. What an opportunity for the gospel! Graham began to see the possibilities, but there was that price tag—$92,000.

Throughout the month, the ad executives called and wired him repeatedly. Each week would cost only about seven thousand dollars, they explained. That shouldn't be too hard to raise. In fact, they felt that if Graham initially raised twenty-five thousand dollars, the network would put him on the air, and then contributions from the radio audience would cover the remainder of the cost week after week.

Again Graham refused. He was overburdened already. When some supporters started a "radio fund" by contributing two thousand dollars, Graham asserted that the final decision was "not mine, but the Lord's." In that spirit he knelt in prayer with Bennett and Dienert, asking God to reveal his will. If twenty-five thousand dollars could be collected by midnight that night, they would believe God was leading in that direction.

Graham was quite sure that would end the matter, unless the Lord performed a miracle. Until then, the largest single gift Graham had received was five hundred dollars. The two ad men left, unhappy with the terms Graham had set. They knew it was impossible to raise so much money in such a short time.

158

This was July 1950, and Graham was in Portland, Oregon, in the midst of his most successful crusade thus far. Some eighteen thousand people crowded into a specially built tabernacle night after night. Before his message that evening, Graham spoke to the overflow audience about the possibility of a nationwide radio broadcast, his repeated refusals so far because of the cost, and his desire to settle the matter according to God's will. "But if any of you folks would like to have a part, I'll be in the office back here at the close of the service tonight."

After the service, Grady Wilson stood at the back office with an old shoe box, collecting money and pledges. An Idaho lumberman put in a pledge for $2,500. People dropped in bills of various denominations. Pledges were scribbled on scraps of paper. An Oregon teacher pledged $1,000, his entire savings, for he "could think of no better investment." When counted, the total was $23,500. Everyone exclaimed, "It's a miracle!" But Graham stood firm. "No, it's not a miracle," he said. "The devil could send us $23,500. It's all or nothing." He had asked the Lord for $25,000 as the indication that the Lord wanted him in radio.

Later, back at the hotel, Wilson picked up the mail at the desk, including three letters for Graham. One contained a check for $1,000, and two held checks for $250 each. Total: $25,000. "Now," Graham finally agreed, "I'll grant it's a miracle."

The Cast-Iron Stove

It was not a good year for J. Hudson Taylor. At twenty-six, he had already been a missionary in China for four years. Yet he was shunned by other missionaries because he dressed in native garb and wore pigtails to identify with the Chinese people. At the time, this was unheard of, but Taylor thought it was an important way to communicate the gospel.

Taylor was also in love with Maria, a twenty-year-old girl. Their relationship wasn't going so well either. Maria's parents had died, and she was now under the care of a spinster who wouldn't let her see Taylor, much less marry him. Despite that,

> The Lord Himself is more than all answers. It is He as relater rather than actor who must take priority in our hearts.
>
> Mike Flynn

the young couple secretly pledged marriage to each other.

After caring for a missionary who was stricken with smallpox, Taylor contracted the disease. By November he was recovering physically, but he and his associate John Jones were in financial distress. Any funds they had were used to provide food to the needy. Now *they* were facing starvation. Their only source of funds was gifts from back home, but the mail was slow and undependable, and no mail delivery was scheduled for another month yet. They needed food *now*.

The two missionaries looked around their house for something to sell. The clock! They took it to a Chinese merchant who promised to buy it. However, he would need to observe it for a week to see if it kept perfect time.

The two missionaries then looked at their stove. It was their one remaining asset. If they could get it across the river, they could sell it as scrap iron to a foundry.

So on January 6, 1858, Taylor and Jones, with no food in their cupboards, decided to sell their stove. Before going out, they prayed the Lord's Prayer. The phrase "Give us this day our daily bread" had extra impact. "Our Father will not forget us," they confidently assured a Chinese helper, but Taylor admitted later, "Our faith was not a little tried."

After prayer they started out, lugging the iron stove with them. Finally they reached the floating bridge across the river, or rather, the place where the bridge was supposed to be. It had been washed out the night before in a violent storm. A ferry was available, but the two didn't have money for the fare. Taylor and Jones looked at each other and then toted the stove back home.

They went to the study "and cried unto the Lord in our trouble." Their Chinese helper ran in while they were still on their knees. "Teacher, Teacher! Here are letters!" No mail was expected for many days yet, but here it was, long before schedule. The letters contained financial gifts for Taylor and Jones.

160

That night Hudson Taylor went to see his fiancée and told her of his financial woes. Maria needed to know that he would always have trouble providing for her. "Don't you see how difficult our life might be?" he said. "I cannot hold you to your promise if you would rather draw back."

"Have you forgotten?" Maria replied. "I was left an orphan years ago, and God has been my Father all these years. Do you think I shall be afraid to trust him now?"

Hudson and Maria married two weeks later.

Running Out of Miracles?

David Wilkerson had no problem dealing with gang members; bankers were more difficult. When a mortgage payment came due on a ministry center in Brooklyn, he needed fifteen thousand dollars. The ministry's bank account only held fourteen. Fourteen dollars.

Many miracles had occurred in the three years since Wilkerson had begun his ministry in New York. Many of these are recounted in the best-selling book (and film) *The Cross and the Switchblade*. God had led him from a small church in Pennsylvania to the violent gang turf of the big city. A number of young gang members had come to Christ, and Wilkerson's work was spreading.

But the impossible mortgage payment was due August 28, 1961. As the date drew near, Wilkerson expected God to do something huge and wonderful to save the center, but nothing happened. The deadline arrived, and they still lacked the money. The bankers were ready to foreclose on the Teen Challenge operation in Brooklyn. Wilkerson worried that he had run out of miracles.

Maybe God wanted him to put more effort into it himself, he thought. So he asked his attorney to seek an extension from the bank. All afternoon the attorney worked on a deal, and finally an extension was granted. The new date was September 10, but that date was final.

God's promises are given not to restrain, but to incite to prayer. They are the signed check, made payable to order, which we must endorse and present for payment. Though the Bible be crowded with golden promises from board to board, yet they will be inoperative until we turn them into prayer."

F. B. Meyer

The attorney asked Wilkerson about his plan to raise the money. "I'm going to pray about it," Wilkerson responded.

So Wilkerson prayed and asked God for another miracle. Then he called together the staff and all the young people in the center— former drug addicts and gang members—and he told them that the center had been saved.

Cheering rocked the place.

"Let's go to the chapel and thank God!" he urged.

They did, praising the Lord for the money. Someone finally asked him where the money had come from.

Wilkerson shook his head. "Oh, it hasn't come in yet, but by September 10 it will come. I just thought we ought to thank God ahead of time."

The early days of September brought no big checks, however. Wilkerson spent hours on the telephone to see what could be done but had no promises of big checks in the near future. He couldn't understand it. During the summer, the response to the ministry of Teen Challenge had been spectacular, touching the lives of twenty-five hundred young people, twelve of whom were now preparing for the ministry.

His board of directors was also phoning friends of the center, but they received only minimal pledges. One of the board members contacted a major donor in Chicago who had given generously in the past, but he couldn't get through to him. Instead, the board member talked to the man's son and asked him to relay the message to his father.

Nothing significant arrived in the mail on the eighth or ninth—only jingling small change.

On September 10, the morning mail arrived. Some of the envelopes contained pennies that children had sent in. Wilkerson thanked God for the pennies, but he needed fifteen thousand dollars.

The midmorning chapel service began with prayer and singing, but everyone was more concerned about what hadn't yet arrived. Some young people, full of faith, were thanking God for a check of fifteen thousand dollars, even though it hadn't come. Then in the middle of the chapel service, Wilkerson was called to the door for a special delivery letter. The postmark said Chicago. He opened it and found a certified check for exactly fifteen thousand dollars.

When Wilkerson returned to the chapel, he couldn't talk. He held up his hand for silence, and suddenly everything was completely still. He handed the check to his treasurer, who in turn handed it to a young boy. "Pass it around," the treasurer told the boy.

It went through the hands of the former gang members, the former addicts, and the Teen Challenge staff members before it returned to Wilkerson.

On the closing pages of *The Cross and the Switchblade,* Wilkerson remarks that the check became "really quite grubby from having passed through the hands of two dozen youngsters who have learned what it is to believe. And perhaps there are a few tearstains on it too."

Building on a Better Foundation

When God doesn't answer our prayers exactly according to our timetable, we often get to experience God in a new and exciting way. That's one of the nuggets of wisdom in Henry Blackaby's popular book *Experiencing God.*

As pastor of the First Baptist Church of Saskatoon in Saskatchewan, Canada, Blackaby had a problem. The congregation was growing too big for its building, a good problem for a pastor to have, but Blackaby knew they'd have to build soon or people would go to other churches with more adequate facilities.

The building fund had only $749. Researching the cost of building, they figured they would need $220,000. A slight shortfall. But Blackaby firmly believed that if God puts it on your heart to do something, you should do it. "Without faith it is impossi-

> "Everything is possible for him who believes."
>
> Mark 9:23

ble to please God," he quoted from Hebrews 11. So he led the people to pray and look to God for the provision. Blackaby was confident "that the God who was leading us would show us how to do it."

What if they provided their own labor? Could they save on construction costs? Could they get started and trust God to provide money for the materials as they needed them? So the project began with the people of the church doing much of the work. And the Lord kept providing the necessary funds. As they were nearing the end of the project, however, they were still about sixty thousand dollars short.

A Texas foundation had promised them money that didn't come through when they expected it. One delay followed another, and Blackaby didn't understand why the Lord was allowing the delays. Blackaby, who had been telling the people to trust the Lord for the provision, was puzzled by it himself. *Why, God, why?*

Then one day when Canada's currency exchange rate with the United States dipped to its lowest point in history, the Texas foundation wired the money to Saskatoon. "You know what that did?" Blackaby noted. "It gave us sixty thousand dollars more than we would have gotten otherwise." The next day the Canadian dollar rose in value again.

"We came to know God in a new way through that experience," related Blackaby. The people marveled that God was caring for a single church while he oversaw the ups and downs of the Canadian economy. But more than that, they learned that "God is far more interested in your having an experience with Him than He is interested in getting a job done. . . . He can get a job done anytime He wants. What is He interested in? You and the world, knowing Him and experiencing Him."

Ask Jesus More Often

If there actually was a Middle of Nowhere, it might be the little village of Aniak, Alaska. But one cold winter, God showed that he was well aware of this place.

Aniak lies on the Kuskokwim River, about halfway between Anchorage and Nome. Seldom are there more than two hundred people in town. In the winter, when the temperature is frequently minus fifty degrees, the population is even smaller.

> God usually gives us our daily bread, not our daily chocolate cake.
>
> David New and Randy Petersen

The Kuskokwim Home was established in Aniak for deserted and native orphan children. It was not a glamorous missionary project, but it was supported by a number of churches in the continental United States and also by the Alaska Native Service before Alaska became a state.

Vera Potter was in charge of the home. She would say that God was in charge, because she had to live by faith month after month.

For several months, she had received nothing from the Alaska Native Service. Her bills were mounting, and she doubted if she could continue heating the Kuskokwim Home. If she didn't pay her bills, her source of food would soon be cut off. Only God could help her now.

So she called the children of the home together and told them that they would all have to pray. She didn't want to scare them, and yet unless God sent some money, the home would be closed down. The children all fell to their knees and prayed fervently. "Help us, Jesus," they pleaded. "You've got to help us."

The next day after lunch, as Vera and some of the children were washing dishes, they heard a knock at the door. The person who knocked didn't wait to be admitted but opened the door himself and entered. Vera and the children knew everyone in Aniak, but this man was a stranger.

The man asked if this was the place where native children were being cared for. Vera answered that it was. And then, as Vera recalls, "he took out a roll of bills and laid them on the table, and without saying anything, he left." They watched as he headed down to the little Aniak airstrip, and five minutes later, he was on the plane that flew him away.

After watching the plane take off, Vera went back to the table and counted the money. It was more than enough for their needs. She told the children that God had miraculously supplied their needs.

One of the little Eskimo boys spoke up. "Aunt Vera, we should ask Jesus for money more often."

Vera never found out who the stranger was or where he had flown from. For her it was enough that the children learned to trust in a God who answered prayer.

Bologna and Burritos

In a way it was garbage day; it was also Christmas. And a Mexican border town had one of the greatest love feasts you could imagine.

Father Richard Thomas of the Lord's Ranch, a Jesuit mission in Mesquite, New Mexico, had been studying Luke 14 with his parishioners, including these verses: "When you give a luncheon or dinner, do not invite your friends, your brothers or relatives, or your rich neighbors" (v. 12). Instead Jesus tells his followers to "invite the poor, the crippled, the lame, the blind" (v. 13).

Many people had been fed at the Lord's Ranch, but Father Thomas didn't feel he had gone to the extremes Christ had urged. So after spending time in prayer, he decided on an outrageous plan—one that might even be outrageous enough for Jesus. On Christmas Day 1972, he and any parishioners who wanted to join him would cross the border to Juárez, Mexico, to the people living in the garbage dumps outside the city. According to the information he had, about 120 people lived in and off of those garbage dumps.

So Christmas Day came. One man brought twenty-five bologna sandwiches to share. Church women made burritos and tamales. Father Thomas supplied a large ham. Others brought little bags of Christmas candy. Then after they had prayed, off they went across the border in vans and trucks to the Juárez garbage dumps.

They knew when they had arrived even *before* they arrived. They could smell the garbage, and they could see the sickly residents of the area scrounging through the garbage for food to eat. Father Thomas had never seen anything like it, people grubbing through garbage for food. One of the church members said it was worse than anything he had seen in the Korean War.

Father Thomas and his people set up folding tables and then brought out the food. At first only a few dozen people gathered, but then more and more came. Instead of a hundred or so people, more than four hundred left the garbage dumps and came toward the smell of the delicious food on the tables.

The priest knew they had a problem—too many people, not enough food. "We'll share what we have," he said. "That's all we can do."

Someone offered him a slice of ham, and he turned it down. "There's not enough," he said, but the person who offered it said, "Yeah, there is." As Father Thomas looked around, he saw everyone with thick slices of ham in their hands. And little bags of candy. Every youngster in the area had a bag, and some had two or three. Father Thomas hollered to the woman in charge of the candy bags, "Jean, we're going to run out of candy if you're not careful." But she could do little about it.

Some of the people came with sacks, which they filled up with food to take home, and then they came back for more. It didn't make sense.

Caught up in the excitement of this most unusual Christmas, Father Thomas was taking photos, not understanding the impossibility of all that was going on.

"It didn't occur to us until afterward that a miracle had happened," one worker said. "We knew what we had taken across and we knew what we had given." Then they realized how many people had been fed and how much food was left over. After everyone had eaten all they wanted, Father Thomas and his friends gathered up what remained—enough to take food to two orphanages that day.

One of the men in Father Thomas's party, Frank Alarcon, was so moved by the miracle of the multiplication of the burritos that he decided to spend his life and his retirement money helping these people in the garbage dumps. He moved across the border to the garbage dumps. Today, on the spot where they set up tables

167

on that Christmas Day, stands a day-care center, a doctor's and dentist's office, and a co-op. The co-op is run by Frank Alarcon, who lives in a one-room house with a mattress on a dirt floor.

"I thank God for that Christmas," says Frank. "It changed my life."

How Did I Ever Get into This?

About fifteen people showed up the first Sunday night Jim Cymbala preached at the Brooklyn Tabernacle. In the middle of his sermon, one of the pews split in half, spilling a third of his congregation onto the floor.

Cymbala knew he wasn't cut out to pastor that church, or any church, really. He was a lot more comfortable playing basketball. In fact, he'd been captain of his University of Rhode Island team, taking them to the NCAA national tournament in his senior year.

Though Cymbala hadn't gone to Bible school or seminary, his father-in-law urged him to come and preach at the Brooklyn Tabernacle, located in one of the sections of the city that few white, middle-class folks would venture into. "They need help," he was told. When he arrived, he realized just how much help they needed.

Despite the pew-splitting incident, the people asked Cymbala to be their pastor. Not sure what he was getting into, he agreed.

Before his first month was up, he realized the church was in serious financial trouble. They needed to pay a monthly mortgage of $232 and had only $160 on hand.

On Monday Cymbala prayed, "Lord, you have to help me. I don't know much—but I do know we have to pay this mortgage." In simple faith, he went to the church on Tuesday, thinking that God would mail in a check; but nothing came. He prayed some more. Then he remembered that the church had a post office box across the street. The needed money must be there. He went there, peeked in the box, reached his hand in, and . . . nothing, absolutely nothing. Discouraged, he went back across the street to the church. He unlocked the door and saw a plain white envelope on the foyer floor. No address, no stamp. Inside he found two fifty-dollar bills, enough to pay the mortgage. Where the money came from, he never discovered.

We demand God's gifts to satisfy our cravings. Yet, only His presence can do the trick.

Leslie Williams

As he and his wife, Carol, continued to minister at the church, they saw some small growth. But Cymbala was getting discouraged. Soon it became "same-old, same-old." Some Sundays he didn't want to show up for the service himself.

While recuperating from a bad cold and lingering cough, he prayed, "Lord, I have no idea how to be a successful pastor," and then it seemed that the Lord interrupted him, telling him that if he and his wife would build the church on prayer, they would lack for nothing. This struggling little Brooklyn Tabernacle would have to be built on prayer. On his first Sunday back in the pulpit, Cymbala told the congregation, "From this day on, the prayer meeting will be the barometer of our church."

Soon people of all races and from all walks of life started coming. In 1977, when their little sanctuary couldn't hold the congregation, they moved to a YWCA auditorium that seated five hundred. Then in 1979, when the YWCA wasn't big enough, they bought a fourteen-hundred-seat theater on Flatbush Avenue and gradually added extra services and started branch ministries.

Carol began to lead and accompany the choir even though she couldn't read music. Most of the choir members couldn't read music either. Yet before long, the Brooklyn Tabernacle choir was putting on concerts at Carnegie Hall, Radio City Music Hall, and Madison Square Garden. The choir's recordings are best-sellers.

What is the secret of the church's success? One of the choir's songs has the line, "If you can use anything, Lord, you can use me." That's the key. Jim Cymbala admitted his own cluelessness, and the Lord answered the prayer he didn't even utter, providing the guidance needed to do God's work in that community.

12

I Didn't Know Angels Looked Like That

God's Messengers at Work in Strange Places

For he will command his angels concerning you
   to guard you in all your ways;
they will lift you up in their hands,
   so that you will not strike your foot against a stone.

Psalm 91:11–12

The Bible tells us just enough about angels to make us want to know more. They are God's secret agents, popping up here and there to do his bidding. They deliver messages, stand guard, and catch stumbling ones. They are called "ministering spirits," sent to serve us.

Angels are often associated with light, sometimes with wings. They are depicted as people in bright clothing. Though they are "spirits," angels generally display a foreboding physical presence; they're always telling people, "Don't be afraid."

Over the centuries, angels have captured the imaginations of many. Some people have created detailed hierarchies of

170

angels. Others have assumed that we become angels when we die. We see pictures of childlike cherubs and movies about angels earning their wings. All of this is make-believe. We must stick with scriptural teaching, even though some questions remain unanswered.

One thing we know is that angels aren't to be worshiped. They worship God like the rest of us. Another thing we can surmise is that angels are sent but not summoned. That is, God sends angels when he wants to; we don't call them to come and help us. Even Jesus refused to create a situation where angels would have to assist him. The scriptural pattern is that people ask God for help directly, and sometimes he uses angels to provide that help.

Still, it's amazing to realize that we have an army of heavenly protectors on our side.

> *Lord, thank you for those angelic bands,*
> *Straight from the King of Kings*
> *That come to bear us in their hands*
> *And shade us with their wings.*
>
> *And thanks for wonders all unseen*
> *Which angels gladly do,*
> *Deliver from the furnace keen,*
> *And safe escort us through.*
> *The Brethren Hymnal (1886)* (adapted)

Undercover Cops under Angels' Care

Two undercover cops were planning a dangerous drug bust, so they prayed first. It was like calling for backup. The response they got was out of this world.

In her book *Where Angels Walk,* Joan Wester Anderson tells the fascinating story of these two policemen, Steve and Phil, of Nutley, New Jersey. Each day before they began their shift, they prayed or read a chapter from the Bible. Often the chapter was Psalm 91, which speaks of God's protection and, in particular, how angels guard us.

Just across the Hudson River from New York City, the town of Nutley had a growing drug problem, and police seemed unable to stop it. Since Steve and Phil looked young enough to blend in with area young people, they were assigned to plain-clothes duty. Soon they discovered a secluded wooded area where teens were buying drugs. What they saw sickened them. "I realized we were not dealing with a few kids having fun," Steve says, "but with many hard-core drug addicts whose minds were out of control." The source of the drugs was a man the officers called Mr. Big.

The next day, after praying again for guidance and the Lord's protection, Steve and Phil returned to the wooded area, following a path that led to a hidden cave, where they found pills, pornographic material, marijuana, and liquor—all the evidence they needed. However, they still needed to catch Mr. Big and some of his key lieutenants, so they decided to wait until evening.

Realizing they would be surrounded by kids, many of whom would be high on drugs, they asked headquarters for extra backup, but that request was denied. Steve and Phil would have to handle it alone. They prayed together again, reminding each other of the promises of Psalm 91.

A crowd of young people near a railroad embankment saw them coming. One girl screamed, "Cops!" Many of the teens scattered, but the policemen caught the girl and called for a backup squad to take her in. Others, they knew, would be in the cave.

Following the path, they soon stood at the entrance of the cave. Steve shouted, "Freeze!" No one moved. About a dozen people were in the cave, including Mr. Big.

When Phil asked Mr. Big to hand over the package he was gripping, he did so very meekly. Those present were told to lie prone on the floor, and they did so with no back talk. The two policemen read them their rights, gathered evidence, and then waited for the police van to transport the detainees to headquarters.

But as they waited, they wondered why there had been no disturbance. The dozen teens surely could have overpowered the two cops as they entered the cave. "Why did the arrests go so easily?" Steve asked Mr. Big as they escorted him to the patrol car.

"Do you think I'm crazy?" he responded. "I saw at least twenty guys in blue uniforms." Mr. Big then turned to another prisoner. "Belinda, how many cops did you see come into the cave?"

"At least twenty-five," she said.

It didn't take Steve long to recall the words of Psalm 91: "You will not fear the terror of night . . . for he will command his angels concerning you to guard you in all your ways" (vv. 5, 11). Over the next nine months, Steve and Phil made 250 arrests, cleaning out the hangouts of drug addicts and vandals in Nutley.

> Prayer is the contrite sinner's voice,
> Returning from his ways;
> While angels in their songs rejoice,
> And cry, "Behold he prays!"
>
> James Montgomery

The Hidden Bible

Dutch watchmaker Corrie ten Boom was fifty-two years old when she was arrested by the gestapo and dispatched to a Nazi concentration camp. The night before her arrest, her family prayed and read together Psalm 91, which contains the verse, "For he will command his angels concerning you to guard you in all your ways."

After being held in two different concentration camps, Corrie was shipped off to the dreaded Ravensbruck in Germany. It was known as the camp from which there was no return. Thus far she had been able to hide her Bible, which was contraband in the camps. Hanging down her back from a string around her neck was a small cloth bag, which contained the forbidden

Bible. That Bible bumping on her back gave her great comfort. "As long as we had that, I thought we could face even hell itself. But how could we conceal it through the inspection I knew lay ahead?"

At Ravensbruck, all possessions were being confiscated, and that meant, unless God worked a miracle, she would have to part with her Bible. Before it was Corrie's turn to be stripped and searched as she entered the camp, she asked permission to use the bathroom. She wrapped the Bible in some extra underwear she had and laid the bundle in a corner. After that initial search, she retrieved the bundle and hid it under the clothes she had been given to wear. It bulged considerably, but she couldn't hide it any better. And there were more searches to come.

So she prayed, *Lord, send your angels to surround me.* Then realizing that angels were spirits, and maybe the guards would see straight through them, she amended the prayer: *Lord, don't let them be transparent today, for the guards must not see me!*

After praying that prayer, Corrie said, "I felt perfectly at ease."

She passed the guards without being touched. Everyone else in line was searched from "the front, the sides, the back." In front of her, a woman had hidden a woolen vest under her dress; it was taken from her. Corrie's sister, Betsie, was just behind her, and Betsie was searched carefully, but Corrie said simply, "They let me pass, for they did not see me."

At the outer door, a second row of guards felt over the body of each prisoner. By this time, Corrie was confident of the angelic protection. "I knew that they would not see me, for the angels were still surrounding me." When they passed her by again, she praised God with the silent prayer, "O Lord, if you can answer prayer like that, I can even face Ravensbruck without fear."

And she did.

At Ravensbruck, more than ninety-six thousand women died, including Corrie's sister, Betsie. In spite of the horror and the terror, Corrie led Bible study groups and clandestine worship services for what she called "an ever-growing group of believers," and her barracks became known as "the crazy place, where they hope." Those guardian angels kept on shielding Corrie and her Bible.

About a week after her sister died, Corrie's name was called during a roll call. She wondered if it would mean added punishment or even the gas chamber. Instead it meant she was being released, set free. Later she found out her release was an administrative mistake.

Corrie ten Boom lived to be ninety-one years old. After World War II, she traveled the world, speaking in more than sixty countries. Her story was dramatically told in the best-selling book and film *The Hiding Place*. Wherever she went, she spread the message that "there is no pit so deep that God's love is not deeper yet."

Guarded by the Lord's Host

From all parts of the world come stories of missionaries who have been protected by angelic hosts.

Billy Graham tells of a medical missionary who was traveling with his family. They were heading home, but it was getting late, so they decided to camp out on a hillside. They knew gangs of bandits roamed the area, but they desperately needed rest. So after praying for the Lord to keep them safe, they went to sleep.

A few days later, the missionary saw a patient at the mission hospital who confessed that he belonged to the bandit gang. The man recognized the missionary from that hillside and asked about the armed regiment that was guarding his family that night. "We intended to rob you," he said, "but we were afraid of the soldiers you had around you—twenty-seven of them."

When the missionary returned home on furlough, he told the story to one of the churches that supported him. Someone consulted the church's records and found they had a prayer meeting that night with twenty-seven people present.

Corrie ten Boom relayed a similar story. Rebels were planning to invade a missionary school in Africa and kill the two hundred students and teachers who were housed there. Knowing of the possible danger, the teachers and students asked God for his protection. The rebel army numbered in the hundreds, but when they got close to the school, they suddenly saw something and fled. The same thing happened a second night, and a third. When one of the rebels was wounded and brought to the mission hospital, he was asked why they had fled. The answer came: "We saw hundreds of soldiers in white uniforms, and we became scared."

From Honan Province, China, comes a story from Rosalind Goforth. She and her husband served there as missionaries in the late nineteenth century. Bandits attacked two Christians in the area and stole their money and possessions, including their clothes. Just as the bandits were starting to leave, the Christians began to pray, asking God to deliver them.

A friend suddenly arrived at the house, and the bandits fled in panic, crying out that they were greatly outnumbered. Quickly, they threw down the clothes, money, and possessions and dashed off.

The robbers told others what had happened. Apparently they saw not just one friend coming, but many others standing alongside him. Rosalind Goforth commented that not only were "these Chinese Christians protected by God in answer to prayer, but from that time on, the violent opposition to Christian activities in the area ceased."

A German missionary told of going into a territory in Indonesia in which two Americans had earlier been killed and eaten by cannibals. He wrote, "Often it seemed as if we were not only encompassed by hostile men, but also by hostile powers of darkness; for often an inexplicable, unutterable fear would come over us, so that we had to get up at night, and go on our knees to pray or read the Word of God, in order to find relief."

After two years, they moved to work with a tribe that seemed more receptive to the Christian message. But soon a tribesman from the previous village came to see him. "I would like to have a look at your watchmen," the tribesman requested.

"What watchmen?" asked the missionary. "I don't have any watchmen."

"Oh, yes, you do. You station them around your house at night to protect you."

The tribesman wouldn't be convinced until he had searched the missionary's house, looking under the beds and in the closets.

"We came together to kill you and your wife," he explained before he left. "But night after night, when we came near, a double row of watchmen with glittering weapons stood close to your home. . . . We went to a professional assassin, who laughed at us because of our cowardice." But when the assassin came to the missionary's house, he too saw the watchmen and ran away.

The missionary then got his Bible and showed the tribesman how God had promised to guard and defend his children.

You Never Know When You Might Need It

"Memorize that verse, because you never know when you might need it." That's what the dean of women had told her.

The verse was Psalm 34:7: "The angel of the LORD encamps around those who fear him, and he delivers them." The school was Pacific Union College, located in Angwin, California, with a population of twenty-seven hundred, more or less, depending on whether school was in session.

177

One of the coeds who memorized the verse was a nineteen-year-old named Charlotte. She worked off campus as a part-time housekeeper, which helped her with tuition, and she traveled back and forth from her housekeeping job by bus. Her life was exhausting—going to classes, taking a long bus ride, working for hours, then taking the bus back to campus. Sometimes at the end of a long day, she simply boarded the bus without thinking.

That's what happened one night, and when Charlotte finally looked out the window and didn't recognize where she was, it was too late to do anything about it. As the bus pulled into a terminal in San Francisco, she knew she was in trouble. San Francisco was seventy-five miles away from the little town of Angwin. And the bus terminal was a far cry from her Christian college. Sailors looked her over very thoroughly. A drunk tried to start a conversation.

Desperately Charlotte looked for someone to help her, but no policeman could be seen. The information booth said: "Closed for the night." On the loading platform, she couldn't see another woman.

This was an appropriate time for that verse in the Psalms to come to her mind. The dean had said, "You never know when you might need it"—well, she knew she needed it now.

Charlotte scurried into the ladies room, locked the door, and dropped to her knees. "I'm lost, Lord, and I'm afraid. Please help me find my way home. You promised to deliver me. Please do it."

When she opened the door and entered the main terminal area again, a young man passed in front of her. It seemed he was carrying a big, black Bible. She was afraid to stop him and ask him anything, but she followed him. Could it be that he was a student at Pacific Union College too? Maybe he was heading back to campus just as she was.

She followed him through several long corridors into an underpass that led to another part of the terminal and then up a flight of stairs. After walking along a dimly lit concourse, she found herself on another loading platform. Then she saw a bus, ready to pull out. Its front sign read, Angwin. The bus was the last to leave San Francisco that night.

The young man seemed to be getting on the bus too. One seat remained and he let her take it. Then the young man turned and got off the bus. Through the window she watched him go. He walked for a few feet and then simply vanished. The lighting was good and yet she couldn't see him. It wasn't that he had blended into a crowd of people—hardly anyone stood on the platform. He had simply disappeared.

Are not all angels ministering spirits sent to serve those who will inherit salvation?

Hebrews 1:14

Charlotte was stunned by it all. It didn't make sense. Then she recalled that verse in Psalm 34: "The angel of the LORD encamps around those who fear him, and he delivers them." The dean of women was right. It was the verse she needed.

Singing in the Skies

"Oh, for a faith that sings!"

It was an unusual prayer for a twenty-five-year-old man to pray.

"Lord, God, give me a faith that will take sufficient quiver out of me so that I can sing! Over the Aucas, Father, I want to sing."

Yes, it was an unusual prayer, but Jim Elliot was an unusual young man. He had prayed that prayer shortly after arriving in Ecuador in 1952 as a missionary to the Auca tribe. Early in 1956, Jim Elliot and four other young missionaries, while trying to make friends with the Aucas, were slain on the banks of Ecuador's Curaray River. The five had just sung a hymn they loved so well they knew it by heart:

> We rest on Thee, our Shield and our Defender,
> Thine is the battle, Thine shall be the praise
> When passing through the gates of pearly splendor
> Victory, we rest with Thee through endless days.

Almost every major newspaper in America announced the tragedy in headlines. National magazines made it their cover story. Jim Elliot's widow, Elisabeth Elliot, wrote the account in *Through Gates of Splendor,* which became a national best-seller. The sister of one of the martyrs continued the work with the Aucas, and many of them turned to God.

Another one of the widows, Olive Fleming Liefeld, returned years later and met the Aucas, some of whom had killed her husband. After telling the details of how the five missionaries were killed, the Aucas said that afterward they heard singing.

"Who was singing?" Olive asked. "The five men?"

"No," one Auca responded, "their dead bodies were lying on the beach."

"So who was singing?"

The missionary translator and the Aucas went back and forth to get a reply to Olive's question. The missionary translator could hardly understand it herself.

Then the translator relayed the Aucas' response. "After the men were killed, Dawa in the woods and Kimo on the beach heard singing. As they looked up over the tops of the trees they saw a large group of people. They were all singing, and it looked as if there were a hundred flashlights."

Olive asked about the word *flashlights* and was told it was the only word for "bright light" they knew.

"And then suddenly the light disappeared."

At first Olive thought the Aucas had just made up that story to please her, but no, the translator said, she had heard the Indians tell stories for many years, and they were always amazingly accurate. If they had just invented the story, Dawa and Kimo would never agree on all the details.

The translator went on to explain that she hadn't talked to them about the killings for a long time, so when Olive went to the jungle to talk about her husband, it was the first chance they had for years to go over the facts.

Had Dawa and Kimo heard angels singing? Were the angels ushering in the five missionaries "passing through the gates of pearly splendor"?

And what about the prayer that Jim Elliot had prayed years before, a prayer the Aucas knew nothing about? *Oh, for a faith that sings. . . . Over the Aucas, Father, I want to sing.*

Not Exactly Angelic Angels

These weren't your typical angels—an opium smuggler, a Chinese bandit, and a Japanese general. But Dick and Margaret Hillis, missionaries in China, accepted their help anyway.

It all started when Dick Hillis was diagnosed with appendicitis. He would have to get to a hospital in Shanghai, which wouldn't be easy.

This occurred in the 1930s, when Japan and China were at war. In order to reach Shanghai, Dick and Margaret and their two children, one an infant, would have to go through the Chinese military lines, through no-man's-land controlled by bandits, and then cross the Japanese lines. To make things even more impossible, it was the middle of winter.

As they left their home, Margaret Hillis prayed, "Lord, let us learn the truth of your promise, 'The angel of the LORD encampeth round them that fear him'" (Ps. 34:7 KJV). While she was praying for the seemingly impossible, she also asked God to supply milk for their baby.

Two days later, they arrived at the Chinese front lines and asked permission to cross. "You're crazy," said the general as he learned of their travel plans. They were asking for certain death. Reluctantly he gave them permission to pass through, but when it came to finding lodging and passage across the Sand River, they were on their own. As they left the Chinese general, they recognized a young man, the son of a Chinese pastor. They knew he had rejected Christianity and was now a drug smuggler, but he was surprisingly friendly. "Can

Prayer can put a holy restraint upon God, and detain an angel till he leave a blessing; it can open the treasures of rain and soften the iron ribs of rocks till they melt into tears—it can arrest the sun in the midst of his course and send the swift-winged winds upon our errand. And all those strange things and unrevealed transactions which are above the clouds and far beyond the regions of the stars shall combine in ministry for the praying man.

Jeremy Taylor

181

All night, all day
Angels watchin'
over me, my Lord.
All night, all day
Angels watchin'
over me.

Traditional
Spiritual

I do something to help you?" He provided them with shelter for the night and helped them find a boat to cross the river.

In no-man's-land the next night, they found an abandoned house and began to settle in. Just then bandits burst in, demanding all their money. Calmly Dick Hillis reached in his wallet, handed one of them his ID card, and asked for the bandit's name. In Chinese, the Hillis name was the same as the bandit's. "Kind sir," said Hillis, "we are members of the same family."

The bandit leader agreed, and he called Hillis his "elder brother," despite the racial differences. That night the Hillises and the bandits slept together peacefully in the abandoned house.

"Do you have any more angels for us, Lord?" asked Dick Hillis as they approached the Japanese lines. Just outside the great walled city of China were the Japanese forces. Sentries placed the Hillises under arrest, putting bayonets to their backs. Unable to speak Japanese, the missionaries were at the soldiers' mercy.

Suddenly three Japanese officers on horseback galloped up. "Where in the world did you come from?" one asked in perfect English.

Hillis told him of his journeys and then asked, "Where did you learn to speak English so well?"

The officer explained that he had attended the University of Washington in 1936. Hillis was amazed. "Then I want you to meet your fellow alumna," he said as he introduced the general to his wife. "She also attended the University of Washington in 1936."

Soon the general was asking what he could do for the Hillises. Margaret asked for milk for the baby. The general told them he would give them a pass through the Japanese lines. He then directed them to a church nearby. "You will find milk at the church. The missionary who used to live there owned a cow."

They got to the church, milked the cow, slept peacefully in the church, and the next day went on their way to the hospital in Shanghai.

Dick and Margaret Hillis laughed later about God's unlikely angels, but they never doubted that the Lord had answered Margaret's prayer.

> They [angels] may be agents to answer prayer, but He [the Holy Spirit] is the Prompter and Director of our prayers.
>
> Fred Dickason

The Bottomless Canyon

Teenager Janie Halliday was vacationing with her brother and sister-in-law in northern Arizona. She left them in the Petrified Forest to get a better photograph. Climbing over a barrier in order to get a good shot, she got as close to the edge of a cliff as she could.

As she edged closer on what seemed to be black ashes, Janie slipped and plummeted downward. Desperately she reached for something to break her fall but found nothing she could grasp. She looked around and saw only the black canyon walls. She looked down, and below her it was black too. The canyon seemed bottomless.

Then suddenly she stopped falling. It seemed as if something or someone had caught her, bringing her to a complete stop. When she reached out, she could touch the slippery canyon walls, but when she tried to turn her body, ever so slightly, she would slide farther downward.

So there she was, helped and yet helpless. She couldn't climb back up—if she tried, she might fall the rest of the way to the bottom. It was a terrifying experience for Janie, but at the same time she felt surrounded by a mysterious presence, as if that presence (whatever it was) was holding her.

Then suddenly she found herself at the top of the canyon again. How she got there, she doesn't know. She knows she didn't climb back up; that would have been impossible. The only explanation she could imagine was that an angel had caught her and carried her safely back up.

When Janie phoned home that evening, she didn't tell her mother about the close call, because she didn't want to worry her. Because Janie didn't say anything, her mother, Shirley, didn't say anything about her own strange experience that day.

In their book *A Rustle of Angels,* Marilynn and Bill Webber tell the mother's side of the story as well as the daughter's. Earlier that day, Shirley had been reading Psalm 91 about how God gives "his angels charge over thee, to keep thee in all thy ways. They shall bear thee up in their hands" (vv. 11–12). Shirley then burst out in tears with a sudden feeling that her daughter was in danger. She prayed, in the words of the *Episcopalian Prayer Book,* "I entrust all who are dear to me to Thy never-failing care and love," and then claimed the promise of Psalm 34:4: "I sought the LORD, and he heard me, and delivered me from all my fears" (KJV). Just as suddenly as she had burst into tears a few moments earlier, she now felt surrounded by peace.

After Janie returned home with her brother and sister-in-law, they showed their photos from the trip. "And here," said Janie, as she passed a photo to her mother, "here is the place I fell." Then the whole story came out.

"Exactly when did it happen?" asked Shirley.

Yes, Shirley had been fervently praying at exactly the time when Janie needed her prayers most.

13

The Touch of the Master's Hand

When God Heals Miraculously

"I am the Lord, the God of all mankind. Is anything too hard for me?"

Jeremiah 32:27

Lazarus died a second time. We don't know when or how, but we can assume that at some later point he took ill and died. Perhaps Mary and Martha prayed for him on that occasion, but he still died. We're not trying to ruin the party, but the truth is that miracles of healing don't always take place when we pray for them. Sometimes God heals people, and sometimes he doesn't.

Of all the subjects we've covered in this book, physical healing is probably the most personal—and the most perplexing. Does prayer have healing power? Absolutely. James says it boldly, "The prayer of a righteous man is powerful and effective" (James 5:16). Centuries of Christian history confirm it. The stories presented in this chapter are just the tip of a vast iceberg.

Yet we mustn't get too programmed by our push-button world. Prayer is not a remote control that automatically clicks on the desired outcome. Yes, it somehow unleashes God's power, but that power has a mind of its own. God has his own purposes. Jesus needed to raise Lazarus the first time to display his power, but later it was time to welcome Lazarus into paradise.

We also must remember that God heals people in many different ways—spiritually, emotionally, and relationally, as well as physically. You'll exult in the amazing physical healing of Barbara Cummiskey when you read about it, but don't miss the spiritual healing that had already been taking place in her life. And don't miss that side of things when you pray for an ailing friend to be healed.

May the power of God preserve me, may the wisdom of God instruct me, may the hand of God protect me, may the way of God direct me, may the shield of God defend me.

St. Patrick of Ireland (adapted)

Drive-by Praying at the Brothels

Sometimes you have a problem that seems so complex you don't know how to pray about it. But you pray anyway, and when God answers, you are amazed at what he did and how he did it. Such was the situation for Pastor Tanto Handoko. Jane Rumph tells about it in her book *Stories from the Front Lines*.

Handoko, pastor of Christ the True Shepherd Indonesian Christian Fellowship in Semarang, Indonesia, faced a crisis. The homes of some church members were surrounded by brothels, because the Sri Kuncoro neighborhood of Semarang had become a center of prostitution. The problem was escalating and Pastor Handoko knew something had to be done.

So the church members prayed—in a unique way. At midnight, at the height of the brothels' thriving business, church members piled into vehicles to drive by the various brothels, praying as they went. They prayed with the authority of Jesus Christ to cast out the demonic force in each place.

Month after month, they continued their drive-by praying. But they couldn't see anything happening; nothing had changed.

Then one day a man asked a colleague of Handoko's to come and pray with his father, who had been suffering from chronic tuberculosis and had been paralyzed for six years. The man lived in the center of the prostitution-infested area.

The colleague, Gaspar Mangke, went and prayed for the man, asking for healing in the name of Jesus Christ. Amazingly the man felt his chest clear and lighten. Then he began to move his paralyzed legs. In astonishment, he exclaimed, "Why, I'm healed."

The next day, the healed man came to church and professed faith in Jesus Christ. Afterward his whole family also came to the Lord. Soon most of his neighbors started coming to church. Friends told their friends what had happened. The impact on the Sri Kuncoro neighborhood was huge.

Within a couple of years, Pastor Handoko had baptized fifty new converts from that area. Some of them had once been prostitutes.

Then Handoko's church established a medical clinic in the neighborhood, and that medical clinic soon became a preaching and Bible study center as well. Today the church continues to grow; more and more new converts are coming to Christ as a dramatic answer to prayer; and the prostitution center is crumbling.

Handoko never imagined that he would have fifty new members, or that his church would open a medical center that would become a preaching center—right in the middle of the problem area. No, sometimes you don't know how God is going to answer prayer. That's what makes prayer so exciting.

The Healing Judge

> "With man this is impossible, but not with God; all things are possible with God."
>
> Mark 10:27

All day long, Judge Kermit Bradford of Atlanta, Georgia, heard cases in his courtroom. He tried to do his part for truth and justice, but he soon learned that some folks needed help far beyond anything he'd learned in law school. Some people just needed prayer.

Judge Bradford became known as a man of prayer. People noticed that God answered his requests, again and again. He never sought publicity, but still the word got out: When all else fails, go to Judge Bradford.

A woman from Waycross, Georgia, did just that. She phoned him one morning as he was about to enter the courtroom.

"Judge, I have a little child that's dying from a brain tumor, and a lady here in town tells me you pray for people. I'm on my way to Atlanta to Eggleston Hospital to have them operate on my child's brain. Is there any way I can see you before I go?"

The judge had a busy day ahead, but he made an instant decision. "Yes," he replied. "Bring the baby down to the courthouse as soon as you can, so we can pray."

She arrived with her eighteen-month-old daughter "hanging over her shoulder like a sack of salt," Bradford noted. The baby's face was almost a sickly green, and its head was enlarged. The mother hurriedly explained that her baby had already been operated on twice, and the doctor had told her a third operation could mean death.

The judge explained to her that God is a healer, and sometimes he chooses to heal through people. When interviewed later, Bradford recalled, "I laid my hands on the little child's head and prayed that God would loose her from this."

After the woman left, the judge mounted the bench and called his court to order, almost forgetting about the sick baby. The next morning, the judge's telephone rang. The young mother was calling with a report on what had happened with her baby.

"We raced down to the hospital," she said. "When the doctors saw that my daughter was near death, they rushed her to the oper-

188

ating room. I waited, of course, to get a report. An hour passed, two hours, and three hours passed; I was pacing the floor."

The mother was worrying that something terrible must have happened—maybe the girl had died in the operating room. Then the doctor appeared, still wearing his mask and scrubs.

"Don't tell me she's dead, doctor!" the mother pleaded.

"No," the doctor assured her. "She is not dead." He explained how they had examined her for three hours. They had taken the previous X rays showing the mass on her brain, and then they made another X ray. The mass wasn't there. It had vanished. Thinking they had made an error, the doctors sent the baby back for yet another X ray, which also seemed to be in error. Finally they had three X rays in front of them. Even a spinal tap showed nothing to be wrong. Then the entire medical staff gathered to tap the child from the top of her head to the bottom of her feet.

The doctor continued, "For three hours we've been trying to work on her before we go into her brain. But the mass is gone, and her head has begun to shrink down from a waterhead to normal. We don't know what has happened. All we know is that she has been healed."

The doctor asked to have the baby brought back in four months for a checkup. Over the next four years, the mother brought the child in for a checkup every four months. The child remained healed.

By the way, the child's father was editor of the Waycross, Georgia, newspaper. He featured the miraculous answer to prayer in large type on the front page: Judge Prays for Daughter and She Is Healed in His Chambers.

Can You Pray for a Horse?

It sounded crazy. Can you pray for a horse? John Wesley, the founder of the Methodist Church, wasn't sure, but he tried it anyway.

Horses were very important to Wesley's ministry. Preaching throughout England and America in the 1700s, Wesley probably traveled 225,000 miles on horseback. "I must be on horseback for life if I would be healthy," he once wrote a friend.

As he rode, he would read with the reins thrown forward onto the mare's neck so the horse could go at its own pace. He said that in riding all those miles, "I scarce ever remember any horse . . . to fall, or make a considerable stumble while I rode with a slack rein." After his seventieth birthday, he often used a carriage for travel, but his preference, when his health allowed it, was to go on horseback.

He followed a tough schedule, waking up each day at four in the morning, and he was just as tough on his horses. On March 17, 1746, after preaching in Newcastle in the far north of England, he was returning on horseback with two companions. They had gone as far as the town of Great Smeaton when one of his companions became ill and had to stop. Wesley continued on, but he didn't know if he could make it to his next preaching mission, because his horse was lame, and he was not feeling well either. He could push himself to go on, but if his horse quit on him, what could he do?

In his diary for Monday, March 17, he wrote: "My horse was exceeding lame . . . he would scarce set his foot to the ground. By riding thus seven miles, I was thoroughly tired, and my head ached more than it had done for some months."

That's when Wesley decided to pray for his horse. Sure it was crazy, but Wesley felt he had to do it. In his diary he almost apologized for his action. "What I here aver is the naked fact: let every man account for it as he sees good."

Wesley then realized the breadth of what God can do. "Cannot God heal either man or beast, by any means, or without any?" He was not just the God of humans; he had made all living things. Even horses. So Wesley prayed for his horse's health, as well as his own, and "immediately my weariness and headache ceased, and my horse's lameness in the same instant. Nor did he halt any more either that day or the next. A very odd accident this."

190

It is not amazing that the founder of Methodism would believe that God can heal, but it is surprising that one of his first prayers for healing was for his horse.

The Pastor Who Lost His Voice

"When you're praying for somebody, don't stop praying, because you don't know when the moment might be that the change will occur. Don't give up."

That's what Duane Miller tells people today, and he knows from experience.

In 1990, as senior pastor of the Brenham, Texas, First Baptist Church, he loved to sing and preach. He had a wonderful family—a loving wife, Joylene, and two college-age daughters.

Early that year, however, with a stuffy head, an achy body, and a sore throat, Miller went to church one Sunday morning and was barely able to get through the two morning services. He went home to bed. First diagnosed as the flu, his ailment was later thought to be a bad case of laryngitis. When he didn't get better quickly, he went to a specialist and there heard the bad news. The specialist said the flu germ had penetrated the protective myelin sheath around the vocal cords and destroyed them. He said the pastor probably would never again have a normal voice.

Miller started seeing other specialists, beginning with a team at Houston's Baylor College of Medicine. One said his problem might be stress related. He should ask for a leave of absence from his church and stay totally silent for six months.

Miller and his congregation prayed for a complete recovery, but none came. In the next six months, his physical condition worsened. Now he had other symptoms, including blurred vision and a loss of equilibrium. Doctors considered other diseases, perhaps multiple sclerosis or epilepsy, but one thing they seemed sure of—within a year or so, Pastor Miller would be completely mute.

With that ominous prognosis, he went to his church and resigned as senior pastor. With a voice no louder than a whisper, he said good-bye to the congregation and then returned to a previous church, the First Baptist Church of Houston, where more friends were praying for him.

Now he had to find a new job, one where speech was not required. Eventually he landed one, doing title research for a federal agency's legal department. But after a few months, he was dismissed for no apparent reason. Everything seemed to be going wrong. Miller's medical insurance coverage was dropped because his doctors had no hope for his recovery. Then his disability income was terminated, because he wasn't completely disabled.

Months passed, then years. Duane Miller was emotionally destroyed, staggering in his spiritual walk. Still, people kept praying for him.

One morning his former Sunday school class invited him to teach their class. It was a ridiculous request. How could he? They told him that they would furnish him with a small microphone, and if he pressed it against his lips, he could make himself heard. With the encouragement of his friends, he said he would try.

It was a large class—about two hundred came to hear him. He croaked into the tiny microphone the text of Psalm 68, which displays the power of God, and then he turned to Psalm 103: "Praise the Lord, O my soul, and forget not all his benefits—who forgives all your sins and heals all your diseases" (vv. 2–3). He stopped for a moment as he read that last phrase, then continued, "who redeems your life from the pit" (v. 4). Again he paused. Now he commented, "I like that verse a lot. I have had pit experiences—we all have had times when our life has seemed to be in a pit."

But as he said the word *pit,* something caught in his throat. People looked up; his voice seemed to be getting stronger. He could hardly believe it himself. "I don't understand what's happening. . . . I'm a bit overwhelmed at the moment. . . . I'm not sure what to say."

The class began clapping and then broke into laughter. Class members came forward to hug him. A miracle had happened.

The doctors couldn't explain it either. They had taken photographs of Duane Miller's throat on every visit and seen scar tissue forming and building up in his throat. Yet when he returned for his next visit, the scar tissue was completely gone. His throat was as healthy as it had been before.

The Case of the Reluctant Healer

Any Bible translator needs a local helper, someone to share the finer points of the language, someone who can test out certain phrasings. Dan Shaw had Hogwanobiayo.

As a linguist with Wycliffe Bible Translators, Shaw had gone to Papua New Guinea to translate the Bible into the Samo language. After he and his wife had moved to the remote village of Kwobi, he quickly made friends with this old tribesman. Hogwanobiayo was probably only fifty, but that was old by Samo standards. He liked the Shaws and "adopted" Dan as one of his "little brothers," though he had no interest in becoming a Christian. He also helped Dan polish his understanding of the Samo language.

When Dan returned from furlough to begin his second term in Papua New Guinea, he heard that Hogwanobiayo was very sick. Not only was Dan worried about the health of this friend, he also realized that without him it would be difficult to finish his translation on schedule.

While Dan was away, Hogwanobiayo had tried everything. His family called in a spirit medium to conduct an all-night ceremony seeking guidance from his ancestor spirits, but no guidance came. He switched beds, believing that "if a spirit who knows where I normally lie down sees me in this weakened condition, I could get attacked while I sleep." Then the entire village danced in drunken revelry all night long hoping to mesmerize the spirits. Nothing worked.

Once, after falling ill, John Wesley took medication for his ailment, but realized he had forgotten something very important:

"I had not yet asked help of the Great Physician, and I resolved to delay no longer. In that hour I felt a change. I slept sound that night and was well the next day."

193

When missionary Shaw returned to the village, he provided some conventional Western medicine, but it didn't help. Village people began referring to Hogwanobiayo in the past tense. They considered him socially dead, beyond hope.

Dan Shaw kept on working with him on Scripture translations, and Hogwanobiayo continued to provide help with the nuances of the Samo language. Then one day Dan needed help on John 5:1–15, the story of Jesus healing the disabled man at the pool of Bethesda. He read the story to the dying Samo tribesman to get his opinion of the translation, but suddenly Hogwanobiayo cried out, "That's me, that's me, that's me."

"What do you mean?" asked the missionary.

"Don't you see?" the ailing tribesman responded. "He tried everything too. He had been sick for a long time, and there was nothing more he could do." Then after another quiet moment, he asked, "Do you think Jesus can heal me too?"

Dan was a linguist, not a healer. He was uncomfortable with the question. He responded cautiously, "Well, yes, Jesus could heal you. He might. It's possible."

Another pause. Then, "I want you to ask Jesus to heal me."

Dan was on the spot. He asked Hogwanobiayo if a Samo Christian should be called in to pray for him.

"No," came the reply. "You're my 'little brother.' I want you to ask Jesus to heal me."

Dan prayed, even though this kind of prayer was hard for him. "Dear Lord, here's my brother, and he needs your healing. He says he believes you can heal him, as you healed the man at the pool. We're asking you to do that right now."

Dan went home to his wife, wondering if he had made a mistake in praying for his friend, because no immediate change had occurred in Hogwanobiayo's condition. But three or four days later, some village children came running to his house, exclaiming, "Come and see. Hogwanobiayo is up and around! He's telling everybody that you prayed for him and Jesus healed him."

Dan went to Hogwanobiayo's house and saw the man walking about for the first time in a month. Dan, with his scientific mind-set, asked, "Are you sure it wasn't the medicine that finally had its effect on you?"

Hogwanobiayo picked up his walking stick and planted it between Dan's ribs. Slowly he asked, "Don't . . . you . . . believe?"

The missionary, now shamed by his own skepticism, responded with tears in his eyes, "Yes, I believe."

The old Samo man instructed the young translator: "Before you prayed, nothing. After you prayed, Jesus healed me."

"You Can't," They Said, but She Did

The downward spiral began when she was in high school. Barbara Cummiskey had been an active teen, playing in the high school orchestra, leading the church youth group, enjoying gymnastics at school.

Then suddenly, "weird things started happening," she says. It wasn't just that she was slipping on the stairs or missing the flying rings in gym class. Soon she had double vision. Before long, she needed braces on her legs, and then it was an arm brace to keep her hands from curling in.

After a battery of tests, the diagnosis was made: "Barbara, you have MS—multiple sclerosis." The doctor told her that nothing could be done. As she got older, she would lose the use of her legs and arms, and then her nervous system would be affected.

The disease indeed progressed as the doctors had predicted. Twice in the next two years, Barbara was rushed to the hospital near death. Sometimes her condition seemed to stabilize, but then the disease erupted again. She began using crutches; breathing became difficult. Soon she needed a catheter and an ilestomy. The pain was so severe that she wore a pain unit, a small device worn on the chest to convert sudden attacks of pain and make them more tolerable.

By the time she was twenty-eight, Barbara was in a wheelchair and needed a constant supply of oxygen. When her diaphragm became infected, the Mayo Clinic told her they were powerless to halt the spread of the disease. What did they sug-

THE TOUCH OF THE
MASTER'S HAND

The healing of the
seamless dress
Is by our beds of
pain;
We touch him in
life's throng and
press,
And we are whole
again.

John Greenleaf
Whittier

gest? She should pray that the deterioration would not continue to spread.

Pray? She had been a Christian since childhood, though at times she had given up on prayer. Sometimes she had questioned God. "I was angry and rebellious at the beginning," she admits.

But now she prayed again. "Please! Please! God, I can't even read your Word anymore. I need something to do." God's answer seemed to be: *Yes, you can do something. Pray for others.*

So Barbara started praying for others. It was the one thing she could still do. When friends came to visit, she asked them to pray with her, and she would pray for them.

Her condition continued to worsen. At thirty, she was technically blind. She needed a tracheotomy to allow more oxygen into her windpipe. Nearly all of her major organs needed assistance to function. "Everyone knew I was dying," Barbara recalls. "The doctors confirmed it."

But as Barbara's physical condition deteriorated, her spiritual condition seemed to become stronger. In the hospital, doctors and nurses were amazed. They didn't know, she says, "how I could turn everything over to the Lord."

Then the following year, a radio program on WMBI in Chicago asked listeners to pray for Barbara—and write to her. She received about 450 letters assuring her that people were praying for her.

The next Sunday, June 7, 1981, as two friends were reading letters to her from radio listeners, Barbara heard a calm, soft voice saying, "My child, get up and walk."

She looked at her friends and said, "I'm not sure what you're going to think about this, but the Lord just told me to get up and walk!" They had not heard anything. Had she gone crazy?

"Get my parents," Barbara urged.

Before her parents could get to her room, Barbara unhooked her oxygen supply and pushed back the covers. "I took a deep breath, and put my foot forward . . . and walked."

Barbara met her mother and father in the hallway. "What a celebration! Just to jump out of bed was a miracle," she recalls, "but I certainly did more than that. Ballet steps and all were tried that day."

One friend, an occupational therapist, said, "But, Barb, you can't." Later this friend admitted, "You just wrecked everything I learned in school. You're absolutely normal."

The next day she went to her doctor's office. "When I saw her walk in," the doctor reported later, "I thought it was some sort of joke, someone dressed to look like Barb. . . . I could not believe it." X rays showed that her lungs were normal again. The doctor took out the tube from her neck and removed the catheter. He found no signs of MS. Other doctors were invited in to verify it.

Her surgeon summed it up: "I realize that there is no medical cure for MS. But at the present time, the patient has no findings of multiple sclerosis, walks normally, speaks normally, and is very happy, as is her family, over the obvious answer to prayer and the good hand of God in her life."

The miracle took place in the 1980s. Two years later, Barbara graduated as a surgical technologist, and today she is a pastor's wife living in Virginia.

The Resurrection of Khev Choen

Only forty years old, he looked more like seventy. Khev Choen had been ill for three years. It wasn't clear what he had, but it had gotten progressively worse. Eventually he was bedridden, then completely paralyzed.

His wife, Jun Mon, knew the end was near, so it was not unexpected when on a late November day in 1993, Khev stopped breathing. She had done everything she could, but herbal medicine and a witch doctor's advice had done nothing to help her husband.

Choked with grief, Jun Mon let her tears flow. Just two weeks before, a ray of hope had entered her life when a small group from a Christian house church had come through her neighborhood, a slum district just outside Phnom Penh, Cambodia. They had shared the gospel with her, and she and her sister had both eagerly embraced the hope of eternal life through Jesus Christ.

But now death had come to her husband. Soon a Buddhist priest arrived with two monks. He checked the body carefully. He had seen many dead bodies before, so he performed the usual ritual and then said, "We'll have to take some of your wooden floorboards to make a coffin, a box for the cremation."

But after the Buddhist priest and the monks left, Jun Mon had another visitor—the woman who had come two weeks earlier to tell her about Jesus. This woman now said that Jesus was the resurrection and the life, and that Jesus had power over death.

That night by candlelight, she and her sister read the verses in the Bible that the woman had quoted. The verses came from the story of the raising of Lazarus. Then Jun Mon began to pray as she knelt near her husband's stiffening body. "Lord Jesus, my hope is in you now. Outside of you I have no hope—my husband is dead. But if you can heal my husband, I will serve you the rest of my life."

For three hours, Jun Mon and her sister prayed. Then about three in the morning, Khev Choen sat bolt upright and shouted, "I'm alive." The two women were terror-stricken.

"I'm hungry," he said. Jun Mon's sister rushed to get him some rice soup, and he ate it. Then he said, "Am I ever glad to be here!"

Jun Mon ran outside and began knocking on doors. She didn't care that it was 3:00 A.M. "My husband is alive," she cried. "Hallelujah!"

About 6:00 A.M., neighbors gathered to see the risen Khev, and about the same time he decided to get some fresh air. As he walked out, the neighbors said, "His ghost is haunting us."

The Christian woman who had first spoken with Jun Mon about Jesus returned the next morning and shared the gospel with her husband. Immediately he committed his life to Christ.

A little home church was started in their house, and within a few months, thirty-two of their neighbors were attending because of the witness of Jun Mon and Khev Choen. Strong and healthy, Khev Choen continued to be a walking testimony to the grace and power of God.

We Can't Spare You Yet

Martin Luther changed the world in dynamic ways, leading the Protestant Reformation that redefined faith, reawakened the public, and redrew the map of Europe. But Luther would have accomplished far less if it weren't for his friend and protégé, Philipp Melanchthon.

The two men were an unlikely pair. Bold and brash, Luther was a bull in a china shop. Melanchthon picked up the pieces and tried to glue them back together. Luther bellowed his opinions while Melanchthon forged compromises. "I am rough, stormy, and altogether warlike," Luther once wrote. "I am here to fight innumerable monsters and devils . . . but Master Philippus comes along softly and gently, sowing and watering with joy."

In many ways, Melanchthon shaped the Protestant movement as much as Luther. Luther challenged his listeners; Melanchthon persuaded them. It was Melanchthon who did most of the writing of the Augsburg Confession, which systematized and filled in the gaps of Luther's teaching.

In the early days of the Reformation, Luther had few friends, and his situation seemed critical. He prayed for hours that God would help him in this time of weakness. When he emerged from his room, he raised both hands and exclaimed, "We have overcome; we have overcome."

This was astonishing. No news had yet been heard to give them hope of relief. But immediately after that, Emperor Charles V issued his Proclamation of Religious Toleration in Germany, a major victory for Luther's side. They *had* overcome.

199

Later, as the Reformation gained momentum, Luther learned that Melanchthon was dying. Luther hurried to be with his friend, finding him in very serious condition. It seemed death could come at any moment.

Melanchthon opened his eyes and looked in the face of his visitor. "O, Luther, is this you?" he said in a whisper. "Why don't you let me depart in peace?"

Martin Luther responded in a strong voice, "Because we can't spare you yet, Philipp. We cannot spare you yet." He dropped to his knees and for nearly an hour prayed for his friend's recovery. Then he sat on the bed and took his friend by the hand.

Again Melanchthon said, "Dear Luther, why don't you let me depart in peace?"

"No, no, Philipp, we cannot spare you yet," Luther repeated. He then ordered some soup. When the soup came, Luther started to feed it to him. Melanchthon turned away and refused to take it. Once again he whispered, "Luther, why will you not let me go home and be at rest?"

"Because we cannot spare you yet, Philipp. Now, take this soup," Luther said more emphatically, "or else . . . or else . . ." He tried to think of something. "Or else I will excommunicate you!"

No doubt Luther was trying to use humor to shake his old pal out of his melancholy. It worked. Melanchthon took the soup and soon regained his health. When Luther returned home to his wife, he told her, "God answered my prayer and gave me my brother Melanchthon."

After Luther's death in 1546, Philipp Melanchthon became the leader of the Reformation. He died fourteen years later at the age of sixty-three.

Go to IHOP

Maybe Irving King wasn't the only frustrated driver on the Connecticut Thruway that day, but he was certainly one of the most bewildered.

He thought he was going on a simple errand. A few months earlier, he had been given a fifty-dollar gift certificate to a sports store in Enfield, Connecticut, and he intended to drive south on Interstate 91 from his home in Massachusetts and buy some sneakers before the gift certificate expired.

Nothing too difficult about that, right? Well, that's what Irving thought too, but he had recently moved into the area, and so he didn't know what exit to take. Exits 47, 48, and 49 are fairly close together, but none of them seemed right to him. He got off one exit ramp after another, but the sports store was nowhere to be seen. He was getting more and more frustrated all the time, and if he was feeling frustrated, he was sure the other drivers on the interstate were probably even more frustrated because of him. Then as he was about to exit again, he thought he heard a voice saying, "Go to IHOP."

Now, Irving King is an evangelist, so you might think he is accustomed to hearing God speak to him like that. But "Go to IHOP" was not the typical divine message, and King was sure that IHOP didn't sell sneakers. For a moment he wondered if IHOP could mean something besides the International House of Pancakes. If it did, he didn't know what it could be. The only IHOP he knew in the area was in West Springfield, Massachusetts, and so, without his sneakers, he headed ten miles north to the West Springfield exit.

In the IHOP restaurant, he was seated in a booth across the aisle from an older woman and a young girl—probably grandmother and granddaughter, he thought. The older woman seemed troubled, maybe struggling with a heavy problem. She looked somewhat familiar; maybe he had seen her before.

Irving asked the woman whether she was a Christian, and she said that she was. He asked if they had met before, and she said she had been to a meeting at which he had preached; afterward he had prayed for her. Irving vaguely recalled praying for her at a church in Springfield.

"But you look worried. Is there a problem? Why are you so upset?"

Then the woman spoke about her daughter—her grand-daughter's mother—who had colon cancer. She had lost forty pounds and was very weak.

Irving had to smile. So this is what the Lord was planning all along. He told the woman, "Funny thing. I went out to buy some sneakers, but couldn't find the place, and instead the Lord directed me here. When I pray for someone's healing, I usually anoint them with oil, but I never take a vial of oil along with me on my daily errands. Today, however, I did."

The woman nodded as if she understood. "This is strange. Two days ago, as I was praying for my daughter, the Lord seemed to say to me that I would meet someone who would pray for her and anoint her with oil."

In his car, he followed the woman to her home. The daughter was obviously in pain; she had difficulty moving around. He talked to her first about her personal relationship to Jesus Christ, and as he prayed with her, she accepted Christ as her Savior.

Then he prayed for her healing and anointed her with oil. Sometimes, Irving said later, he senses the Spirit of God as he anoints someone and prays for healing, and he sees instantaneous relief. In this case, he felt no presence of God; instead, he seemed to feel the cold blackness of death. As he left the house, he felt that maybe the purpose of his strange calling to IHOP was to lead this young mother to Christ but not for her physical healing.

A few days later, he called the grandmother to check on her daughter's condition.

That very day, the daughter had been examined in the hospital. No trace of colon cancer was found. She had been healed, the grandmother said, and was now telling everyone she met what God had done.

As for Irving King, he will never forget the day God said, "Go to IHOP." But whether he ever found the sports store to get his sneakers, we don't know.

14

When Even the Road Map Seems Mixed Up

How God Opens Doors When All You See Are Walls

> Trust in the LORD with all your heart
>   and lean not on your own understanding;
> in all your ways acknowledge him,
>   and he will make your paths straight.
>
> Proverbs 3:5–6

"Where do you want to go today?"

A computer company used that simple question to illustrate the unending potential of its products. With the right connections, the right computer can take you virtually anywhere.

We can share with God the same question each morning, with some possible variations. Where do you want me to go today? Where shall I take you? Where will you take me? Our lives with Christ are abundant because God's mercies are new every morning. We never know what he's going to do next.

The Bible speaks of the Christian's life as a "walk." Not a "sit" or a "recline." We're on the move. When we're walking with Jesus, step-by-step, great things can happen. As we walk, we talk, and he teaches us and guides us and helps us grow more like him.

Some of the answered prayers you'll find in this chapter don't sound like prayers. They're more along the lines of "Where do you want to go today, Lord?" God answers these prayers not by giving us something we want, but by guiding us in the way that he wants. Our lives are all the richer.

Quiet Time

Oh, God, I can't—
You never said I could,
Oh, God, You can —
You always said You would.

Author Unknown

Tall Order for a Little Woman

She had no business thinking that she could ever be a missionary. Gladys Aylward, barely five feet tall, had been a shopgirl, a nanny, and a parlor maid. The daughter of a mailman, growing up near London, England, Gladys had only a basic education. She was hardly a candidate to learn a foreign language and become an effective foreign missionary, and certainly not a missionary to China, halfway around the world.

One day while riding on a bus, she read a story about China and the need for missionaries there. She had been converted to Christ at the age of eighteen, but now ten years later, she felt God was asking her to volunteer for missionary work in China. So she applied to the China Inland Mission. She was rejected because of her lack of education.

Disappointed, Gladys went back to her servant's room and emptied her purse on top of her Bible. Two pennies fell out. And then she prayed, "O God, here's my Bible! Here's my money! Here's me!"

It was an odd kind of prayer, maybe more of a challenge, but it showed her faith in God's power. She believed that somehow God would get her to China, as unlikely as that seemed to be.

> Pray continually; give thanks in all circumstances, for this is God's will for you in Christ Jesus.
>
> 1 Thessalonians 5:17

When she heard that a small independent mission in North China needed a worker, she determined to become that worker. But how?

She saved every penny she could. Traveling by ship would be too expensive, so she decided to go overland by Trans-Siberian Railway across Europe and Asia and through a war zone on the Manchurian border to her destination.

So on October 15, 1932, thirty-year-old Gladys Aylward went to London's Liverpool Street Station to begin her journey. A small group of her friends waved good-bye. She nearly lost her life on the trip, but she made it to remote Yengcheng, showing up at the doorstep of an older missionary who didn't know what to do with her. That missionary died within the year, but in that year they had opened an inn for Chinese muleteers (mule drivers).

Gladys had to learn the Chinese language by herself, but she did so by listening to the mule drivers talk. Then the mule drivers began listening to Gladys talk. She told them Bible stories, and her Inn of the Sixth Happiness gained popularity because of her skill as a storyteller. To support herself, she worked for a local official who appointed her Inspector of Feet. The official had been campaigning against the ancient practice of foot-binding girls, and she was glad to help him in his campaign.

In 1940 when the Japanese invaded Shanghai, Aylward led one hundred children on a long journey to safety. The heroic story was dramatically told in the popular film *Inn of the Sixth Happiness*.

Prayer is the offering up of our desires unto God, for things agreeable to his will, in the name of Christ, with confession of our sins, and thankful acknowledgement of his mercies.

Westminster
Assemblies of
Divines

When illness forced her to return to London, Gladys dined with England's nobility and with Queen Elizabeth herself. She spoke to the largest churches of the land.

Gladys Aylward knew her own limitations. In fact, she felt, "I wasn't God's first choice for what I've done for China. There was someone else. . . . I don't know who it was—God's first choice. I don't know what happened. Perhaps he died. Perhaps he wasn't willing. And God looked down . . . and saw Gladys Aylward."

That's what she thought, but a lot of others thought that Gladys Aylward was God's first choice all along.

Betty Greene and Her Flying Machine

Flying for God? It was a strange idea, and Betty Greene wasn't sure what to do with it. She had been fascinated with planes as a teenager, and now she wondered what to do with that passion. At twenty years of age, she was looking for a good way to serve the Lord with her life, but how? Finally she prayed, "God, I've never heard of anyone who used flying to help spread the gospel message, but if you want me to fly for you, show me how to make it happen."

Four years before that prayer, she had flown in an airplane for the first time. In 1936 Betty had been given the ride as a present on her sixteenth birthday. Then when an uncle gave her a birthday gift of a hundred dollars, she invested in flying lessons. Before long, she was flying solo.

As she approached college graduation, none of her career options excited her—nothing but flying. But what could she do with that? She confided her frustration to a family friend, who told her, "I think God plants his desires in our hearts and wants us to act on them."

So Betty went to God and poured out her problem. She knew the whole idea was preposterous. How could you fly for God? Even if it were possible, wouldn't that be a job for a man, not a woman?

When World War II broke out, the military formed a small group of women pilots. Their job was to ferry planes back and forth, releasing male pilots to fly combat missions. Soon Betty was a member of the WASPs (Women Airforce Service Pilots). As a WASP, she flew a variety of military aircraft, including developmental projects like the four-engine B-17 Flying Fortress.

When the WASPs were disbanded, Betty heard of a new mission organization that some Christian men hoped to start. It had no staff and no budget, but it did have a name—the Christian Airmen's Missionary Fellowship (later known as Missionary Aviation Fellowship). Because no male pilots were available yet (they were all still fighting in World War II), Betty Greene set up the new organization's headquarters. Early in 1945 she bought an airplane for the infant organization, and MAF was in business.

Today MAF operates the world's largest nonprofit fleet of private aircraft used for the public good. Its seventy-five planes annually log more than forty-five thousand flights to more than three thousand grass or dirt airstrips, traveling nearly five million miles a year. MAF serves more than five hundred Christian and humanitarian organizations, delivering supplies and personnel to hard-to-reach places.

What an amazing answer to a frustrated coed's prayer: "God, I've never heard of anyone who used flying to spread the gospel message, but if you want me to fly for you, show me how."

With a Baseball Bat in His Car

The two things Dick Musielak wanted more than anything else were physical restoration for his twenty-three-year-old son's

> Do not pray for easy lives,
> Pray to be stronger men.
> Do not pray for tasks equal to your powers,
> Pray for powers equal to your tasks.
>
> Phillips Brooks

mangled body and revenge on the thugs who had done that to him. Neither of the two was happening, however, and Musielak got madder and madder.

Since he had first seen his son in the hospital bed, he had craved revenge. His son had merely stopped at a convenience store on his way home from work and ended up beaten and bloodied by thugs.

"Paul looked like a piece of raw meat that had just been slaughtered," Musielak recalls. Doctors suspected brain damage. His vision might be permanently damaged, they said. X rays showed a skull fracture, as well as fractures of the nose and orbital bone. Who wouldn't want revenge?

All Dick Musielak could think of was how to get the goons who did it. He tacked up "wanted" posters, he offered rewards for information, and he put a baseball bat in his car. Meanwhile, his son lay in the hospital bed, showing no improvement.

Then one Sunday at church, Dick found it hard to concentrate on the sermon. He was thinking of the baseball bat in his car and what he would do if and when he caught those responsible. Although his mind wandered, he heard enough to know what the minister was talking about, and he didn't like the subject. The text had something to do with forgiveness, of all things. Then he heard the words of Jesus: "Forgive your enemies and pray for those who mistreat you."

Pray for them? How could he? Almost out loud he said, *Not today, Lord.*

When the minister quoted other passages, Dick Musielak felt like getting up and walking out. But what really got to Musielak was when the minister quoted Jesus' words, "And when you stand praying, if you hold anything against anyone, forgive him, so that your Father in heaven may forgive you of your sins" (Mark 11:25).

It hit him like a ton of bricks. If he kept holding such bitterness in his heart, he couldn't ask God to heal his son. His

208

own heart had to be healed before his son could be healed. He didn't think it made sense at first, but nothing else seemed to be working.

And so as he sat in the pew, he began to pray silently, *O God, help me. Help me to forgive those people, whoever they are. Please take these awful feelings from my heart.* As he prayed, tears of release came to his eyes. He was no longer bound by hatred; a wave of peace swept over him. Now he prayed for his son and for his son's attackers as well.

After church he went back to the hospital. A nurse met him coming out of the elevator. "Mr. Musielak," she said, "it's your son. We don't know how to explain it." Fearing the worst, he rushed past her and into his son's room. There he was, sitting up in bed. New X rays showed no signs of a fracture. His eyes were bloodshot, but there were no scars or even bruising.

The doctors had no answers. They shook their heads in amazement.

The next day Dick and his wife checked the doctor's exit report on their son. X rays on Saturday clearly showed evidence of a fractured skull and brain damage, but on Monday there was no sign of a fracture at all. On Saturday he had been treated for deep lacerations and was given the prognosis of permanent disfigurement and possible future blindness. On Monday he left the hospital as if nothing had happened.

And Dick Musielak never used the baseball bat in his car.

Is Now the Time to Turn Back?

The man's flight was delayed. Of course that meant he'd miss the connecting flight in Cairo, and who knew when he'd get to Ethiopia? Certainly not in time for his important meeting. Many choice words have been uttered by various travelers in similar situations over the years, but this man chose to utter a prayer: "Dear Lord, shall we try to go farther on this journey, or is now the time that we should turn back?"

> The LORD will guide you always; he will satisfy your needs in a sun-scorched land.
>
> Isaiah 58:11

V. Raymond Edman, president of Wheaton (Illinois) College, had been invited by Haile Selassie, emperor of Ethiopia, to come to Africa and evaluate his educational system. Yet his travel plans were going awry. Edman, accompanied by Dr. E. Joseph Evans of Boston, stood by the counter of the airline's downtown ticket office in Athens, Greece, and wondered what to do. "I needed to know the mind of God right then and there," he said. They would have to return to America if they couldn't catch a plane soon.

This occurred during the years immediately after World War II, when airline connections were often atrocious. If you missed a flight, you could never be sure how long you would wait for another plane headed for your destination. The missed connection in Cairo might mean a delay of a week or more. "We were scheduled to fly early that Monday morning from Athens to Cairo and from there to Addis Ababa, the capital of Ethiopia," Edman recalled later. At the Ethiopian Embassy in Cairo, they would be able to pick up their Ethiopian visas, but the problem was that only one plane a week went from Cairo to Addis Ababa, and that plane was scheduled to depart at four o'clock Wednesday morning. They needed all of Tuesday to secure their visas and make other arrangements.

When they learned of the flight delay on Monday morning, they were told to be ready because the flight could depart at any time. "All day long we waited for the word," Edman said, but no word came. They returned to their hotels and waited; they were told that they would be phoned if the plane was available. Early Tuesday morning they again reported to the airport, where they were told that the plane still had not left Rome en route to Athens. Time was running out.

Noon came, and still there was no word. When afternoon came, Edman realized that it would be impossible for them to get to Cairo in time to get their visas. So the two travelers prayed. It would certainly be disappointing to turn back at this point, but on the other hand, they couldn't afford to spend a whole week waiting for the next plane. Perhaps they had been mistaken in accepting the invitation to Ethiopia. Was God preventing them from doing something that was not his will?

Then Edman says, "Quietly in the depths of my heart was the impression: Go as far as you can!" He took it as an assurance that they were in the right place, and they'd just have to trust God for the next leg of the journey. "Thus far we knew that we were in the center of God's will."

> We precede, enfold, and follow all our work with prayer. Prayer and action become one.
>
> Richard J. Foster

Not long after they prayed, they got word that the plane would soon be arriving from Rome and would quickly be dispatched to Cairo. They boarded the aircraft, still not sure how they would get to their appointment in Ethiopia. When they arrived in Cairo about 9:30 P.M., the big Trans World Airlines plane parked right next to a little C47 with a lion painted on the side—the sign of the Ethiopian Airlines!

It was good to see that small Ethiopian Airline plane there, but they still had no visas. As they stood in line to have their passports stamped, a TWA agent asked about their travel plans. When they told him their situation, he responded that he himself would arrange for the transfer of their baggage to the Ethiopian plane and would see them off at four o'clock the next morning. "You won't need the visas," he said. And that's what happened.

"We had gone as far as we could," Edman said, and then the Lord opened the doors for them to go the rest of the way.

Mr. Creator, Who Made the Peanut?

"What makes grass green?"

"What makes grasshoppers jump?"

These and many other questions filled the mind of young George Washington Carver. Once when his foster parents were planning to visit a man who had the best vineyard in the area, ten-year-old George asked, "Why are grapes purple?"

Pray with pencil and paper at hand. When God sends a thought, write it down and keep it visible until it can be carried into action.

Bill Hybels

"I don't know," said his foster father. "Nobody knows."

"Does God know?" the boy wondered.

"Of course he does," came the reply.

"Then I'll ask him," responded the boy, and he left the room.

The foster father was bothered by the boy's attitude. "He shouldn't talk that way," he growled to his wife. "He sounded as if he were going to meet God out there—around the house."

The farmer's wife answered quietly, "Maybe he will."

The boy who asked too many questions and carried on conversations with God became a world-renowned botanist. He is best known for his work with peanuts and sweet potatoes, from which he was able to develop more than four hundred synthetic materials, including dyes, soap, cheese, and a milk substitute.

At the turn of the twentieth century, peanuts had been a minor crop in the South, but by 1923, after George Washington Carver's discoveries were publicized, fifty-three million bushels of peanuts were being grown each year.

In a lecture once, this African-American scientist described the conversation with God that got him started studying the peanut.

I asked, "Dear Creator, please tell me what the universe was made for?"

The great Creator answered, "You want to know too much for that little mind of yours. Ask something more your size."

Then I asked, "Dear Mr. Creator, tell me what man was made for."

Again the great Creator replied, "Little man, you still ask too much. Cut down the extent of your request and improve the intent."

So then I asked, "Please, Mr. Creator, will you tell me why the peanut was made?"

"That's better, but even then it's infinite. What do you want to know about the peanut?"

"Mr. Creator, can I make milk out of the peanut?"

"What kind of milk do you want, good Jersey milk or just plain boarding-house milk?"

And then the great Creator taught me how to take the peanut apart and put it together again.

George Washington Carver, who became America's foremost agricultural scientist, freely offered the secret of his success. He said, "A personal relationship with the great Creator of all things is the only foundation for the abundant life." Then he added, "Walk and talk with God and let him direct your path."

Getting Away from It All

Christine Wood was running away. Life was full of problems and questions, and she was finding no answers in the little English town where she lived.

She wasn't sure that God was interested in her anymore. She had certainly prayed enough, but was God listening? Maybe her problems were too big for him to deal with.

Christine decided to go to Switzerland and relax on the shores of Lake Geneva. "I spent many hours beside the lake," she recounted in an article in *Decision* magazine, "drinking in the serenity and gaining inspiration from the grandeur of the mountains on the far shore." God was there too, waiting to reveal himself. Soon she felt at peace with all the world.

When a storm arose and lightning ripped through the sky, she felt it was God assuring her of his power. When she saw a rainbow at the far end of the lake, she was sure that it was God's promise that he was watching over her.

But then she returned home, where her troubles were; they hadn't disappeared. Living with her parents, who were always shouting at each other, Christine felt she was being blamed for everything.

Unable to tolerate her home situation any longer, she had to move out but had nowhere to go. Her finances were meager,

> It's the quiet moments after prayer that really matter. They nourish authentic Christianity. Power flows out of stillness, strength out of solitude. Decisions that change the course of lives come out of these quiet times.
>
> Bill Hybels

and apartments were scarce and expensive. Her health was going downhill; she sought the counsel of a hospital specialist who told her that she must leave home or else she would have both a physical and emotional collapse.

That night by her bed, she agonized, "Please God, you *must* help me!" She tried to think back to her experiences at Lake Geneva—God showing his power in the lightning and his care for her in the rainbow. But now all that seemed long ago and far away.

How could God find an apartment for her? "Would he drop a flat down from heaven by parachute just for me?" Even the thought of it seemed irreverent, and she was more in despair than ever.

That night she talked to a friend, who said, "You know, it may be that God won't lead you to another home just because you want to go. . . . He will move you when you really need to go."

"But I need to go now," Christine replied. "The doctor says so."

"Maybe God will never move you," said the friend, who went on to suggest that the difficulties she was facing could strengthen her.

It was a message Christine didn't want to hear. But then she thought back again to her Lake Geneva experience. At the lake she had endured the storm, because God was revealing his power in the storm. Maybe now, if she endured the personal storm, God would reveal himself to her again.

That night she slept better than she had in months.

A few days later, she received a phone call from a former employer. "Still looking for a flat? One of mine has unexpectedly become vacant."

She hurried to take a look, and it was love at first sight. "I felt as if a little bit of heaven had suddenly come to earth for me," she said.

And later she wrote, "Of course God loved me! Of course he cared! He had been with me in the storm. He knew how much I could take and asked no more."

The Rise of a Rose

It looked as if Rose Hawthorne Lathrop would gain the same literary stardom that her father had. Nathaniel Hawthorne, perhaps America's greatest nineteenth-century novelist, had become famous for *The Scarlet Letter* and *The House of the Seven Gables*. Now his daughter Rose was moving in the same literary circles, with stories published in the *Atlantic Monthly* and other national magazines. A volume of her poetry was well received by the literary critics.

But things turned sour for Rose. Her husband became an alcoholic. Their only child died at the age of five. Her good friend Emma Lazarus, the author of the lines later inscribed on the Statue of Liberty, "Give me your tired, your poor, your huddled masses . . . ," was dying of cancer.

Rose realized that although she was suffering and grieving, others suffered far more than she did. Then her minister told a story that she could not forget.

He told of a young seamstress, a sensitive and cultured woman, who was suffering from cancer. Cancer was a mysterious disease at the time and many thought it might be contagious. So this seamstress was evicted from her room. She spent her life savings trying to find a cure. She was admitted to a private hospital, which transferred her to the city hospital when her savings were gone, and from there she was sent to a poorhouse on Blackwell Island, where she lived, alone and friendless, with murderers and rapists. She died in despair, and her body was dumped in a pauper's grave.

Rose couldn't get the story out of her mind. She began to pray over and over again, "God, help me to help them."

It seemed impossible for her to help cancer sufferers. She was neither a doctor nor a nurse and had little money. So it

My life is one long, daily, hourly record of answered prayer for physical health, for mental over-strain, for guidance given marvelously, for errors and dangers diverted, for enmity to the Gospel subdued, for food provided—for everything that goes to make up life and my poor service.

Mary Slessor

seemed unlikely that God could answer her prayer to "help me help them."

As she kept on praying this prayer, she got an idea. She would somehow rent some rooms in the poorest part of town and offer free nursing to poor and homeless women. Because she knew nothing about nursing or about treating cancer, she volunteered at a hospital to learn what she could. At first, the sight of some of the cancer patients sickened her, but gradually she was able to muster her courage and treat the cancer patients who came to her.

Taking a house in the slums, Rose began writing again to fund this project. She published a paper called "Christ's Poor" to promote the work. Her first cancer home was a three-room slum apartment that sat between horse stables.

In 1900 she and a friend started the Servants of Relief for Incurable Cancer. The work grew and moved several times to larger facilities. There were always more cancer patients than she could provide for. She prayed for more space, and then she was offered an old hotel on nine acres just outside New York City. Today, the work begun by the woman who prayed, "God help me to help them," operates seven such homes in six states, serving poor incurable cancer patients of all races and denominations.

When Rose died in 1926, her minister said, "I do not exaggerate when I say that she could have taken her place in the chronicles of American literature, but she sought higher things. Her mind flew to God. She gave it to him, she diverted it to his purposes, and he accepted it, and she loved him with her whole mind."

The Hills Are Alive

The hills weren't always alive with the sound of music. In fact, *The Sound of Music* never would have happened if it weren't for an answer to prayer.

When Maria von Trapp was a young novice at a Benedictine abbey in Austria, she told her Mother Superior that she thought the most important thing in life was "to find the will of God and do it."

The Mother Superior questioned her further, "Even if it is hard?"

Maria quickly responded, "Of course, even if it is hard." At the time, however, she had no idea how hard it might be.

Maria had been selected to become a teacher for the seven children of Baron Georg von Trapp, a navy captain. In the baron's home, she taught the children how to find God's will and do it. She said later, "Doing God's will became second nature in our whole family." Maria fell in love with the children and also fell in love with Baron von Trapp, later marrying him.

When Hitler invaded Austria, the von Trapp family hoped at first that the Nazi occupation wouldn't affect them. But as the children were told to spy on other children, as reading material was censored, as the Nazis intruded more and more into their lives, Maria said, "There was no question where the will of God was leading us. We saw we could not stay." So they left Austria, fleeing across the Alps through a tunnel into Italy.

But now, what could they do to survive as a family? Von Trapp was a naval officer and a member of the Austrian nobility; he had no particular skills that would help him provide for his family.

Maria and the children prayed for God's guidance. "The only thing we could do well together was sing; it was our family hobby," Maria said. But the baron was against the idea of his family going on stage. Eventually, however, they all felt it was God's will for them, and so they tested it out. At first they sang at small parties and performances that hardly earned enough to put food on the table. Then they performed concerts. And then they sang on the Italian opera circuit in Florence, Milan, and Rome.

They looked for other things they could do, but as Maria said, "God closed all of the other doors."

When it is difficult to know God's will, Maria said, then eliminate all the possibilities except one, even if it goes against your grain. "Then you are left with what God wants. And you set your teeth and with a big sigh, you do it. If that choice truly is God's, then peace, security, and joy—not anguish and unhappiness—will follow."

For twenty years the von Trapp family earned a living by presenting concerts, traveling all over Europe and then emigrating to the United States. They eventually became quite famous. *The Sound of Music,* one of the most beloved musicals and movies of all time, was based on their story. And the Trapp Family Lodge in Stowe, Vermont, became a popular year-round resort for vacationers.

The key to it all, said Maria von Trapp, is to start each morning by asking the Holy Spirit for guidance. "I ask for guidance and offer up everything that will happen during the day as it comes. I renew my strength to do his will."

Acknowledgments

In addition to personal contacts by letter, phone, and e-mail, we searched hundreds of books and magazines as we prepared these amazing answers to prayer. Listing all the sources of our research would be difficult, but we want to acknowledge the following books and magazine articles that were extremely helpful. All the stories were completely rewritten, and while we tried to verify the material, any mistakes are ours and not that of the original source or sources.

The following notes and acknowledgments are given by story title in the order in which they appear in the book.

Chapter 2: Prayer in the Hot Spots

"Kabul: Unlocking the Taliban Prison"—Written from various news sources as well as information from Antioch Community Church, Waco, Texas.

"Oklahoma City: 'I Couldn't Outrun Prayer'"—A more complete story can be found in Jim and Karen Covel and Victorya Michaels Rogers, *The Day I Met God* (Sisters, Ore.: Multnomah, 2001).

"East Germany: Why the Wall Came Tumbling Down"—Based on material in Philip Yancey, *Finding God in Unex-pected Places* (Nashville: Moorings, 1995).

"Beirut: 'It Was Just God and Me'"—The full story is in Ben and Carol Weir, *Hostage Bound, Hostage Free* (Philadelphia: Westminster, 1987).

"Pearl Harbor: 'Father, Forgive Them'"—Background information from David Seamands, "The Kamikaze of God," *Christianity Today*, 3 December 2001, 58.

"Moscow: 'What a God We've Got'"—Based on material in Jerome Hines, *This Is My Story, This Is My Song* (Old Tappan, N.J.: Revell, 1968).

"Pray for the Miners"—Written from news stories in various newspapers, news magazines, and Internet sources.

"Cape Town: The End of Apartheid"—Background can be found in Desmond Tutu, *No Future without Forgiveness* (New York: Doubleday, 2001) and Shirley De Boulay, *Tutu: Voice of the Voiceless* (Grand Rapids: Eerdmans, 1988).

Chapter 3: Surprise, Surprise

"Moving a Mountain by Faith"—Based on story in Russell T. Hitt, *Sensei* (New York: Harper and Row, 1965).

"Rhoda's Big Surprise"—This story is much better told by Luke in Holy Scripture, Acts 12:1–19.

"Prayer Answers by the Bunch"—The complete story can be found in Darlene Deibler Rose, *Evidence Not Seen* (San Francisco: HarperSanFrancisco, 1990).

"Russian Room Service"—Based on material in Jane Rumph, *Stories from the Front Lines* (Grand Rapids: Chosen, 1996; Fairfax, Va.: Xulon, 2001). Used by permission of the author. All rights reserved.

"When God Healed a Windmill"—Based on material in Rumph, *Stories from the Front Lines.* Used by permission of the author. All rights reserved.

"The Mysterious Phone Booth"—Based on material in Ken Gaub, *God's Got Your Number* (Green Forest, Ark.: New Leaf, 1998), as well as other sources. Used by permission.

"Les Lemke's Hidden Talent"—The story is told in full in Pat Robertson and William Proctor, *Beyond Freedom* (New York: William Morrow, 1985).

"Miracle Well in the Persian Desert"—From the Evangelical Press News Service, 4 September 1992.

Chapter 4: Look What You Started

"They Weren't Known for Their Praying"—Rewritten from the first two chapters of the Book of Acts in the Bible.

"Two Women of the New Hebrides"—A more complete story can be found in Elmer Towns and Douglas Porter, *The Ten Greatest Revivals Ever* (Ann Arbor, Mich.: Vine, 2000).

"The Man Who Revived New York City"—Based on information from many sources, including Keith J. Hardman, *Seasons of Refreshing* (Grand Rapids: Baker, 1994).

"Ola Culpepper and Her Optic Neuritis"—Based on material in Lewis and Betty Drummond, *Women of Awakenings* (Grand Rapids: Kregel, 1997).

"From Soles to Souls"—Derived from several Moody biographies, including Richard K. Curtis, *They Called Him Mister Moody* (Grand Rapids: Eerdmans, 1962).

"The *C* in YMCA"—Derived from John Pollock, *A Fistful of Heroes* (Fearn, Ross-shire, Great Britain: Christian Focus, 1998).

"Something Too Big for Us"—Derived from various sources, including John Pollock, *Billy Graham* (Grand Rapids: Zondervan, 1966).

"Bibles and Wild Turkeys"—Derived from several sources, including Robert J. Morgan, *More Real Stories for the Soul* (Nashville: Thomas Nelson, 2000).

"What They Found in a Haystack"—Derived from several sources including Peter Marshall and David Manuel, *From Sea to Shining Sea* (Grand Rapids: Revell, 1986).

Chapter 5: Long Distance, Please

"Kidnapping in the Ivory Coast"—Information from Baptist Press News Service, 25 May 2000.

"The Spiritual Power of a Bedridden Girl"—Derived from G. Campbell Morgan, *The Practice of Prayer* (Old Tappan, N.J.: Revell, 1905).

"The Sinking of the *Titanic*"—Condensed and adapted from Robert J. Morgan, *More Real Stories for the Soul* (Nashville: Thomas Nelson, 2000).

"Stay in the Net"—The story was told in the media as well as in General and Mrs. James L. Dozier, "A Story of Answered Prayer," in *The Miracle of Prayer* (New York: Crescent, 1991).

"A Verse for Vietnam"—Background material from Jim Stegall, "Hardly a Coincidence," in *Changed Lives—USA Testimonials* (Nashville, Tenn.).

Chapter 6: Just in the Nick of Time

"Saved by a Cloud"—Based on a story in John Van Diest, comp., *Unsolved Mysteries* (Sisters, Ore.: Multnomah, 1997), but the original source of the material is unknown.

"The Miracle at Valley Forge"—Much of the information can be found in David Balsiger, Joette Whims, and Melody Hunskor, *The Incredible Power of Prayer* (Wheaton: Tyndale, 1998).

"Livingstone's Lion"—Background information from David Livingstone biographies and from Basil Miller, *Answered Prayers on the Mission Field* (Grand Rapids: Zondervan, 1955).

"The Rescue of 'Hernia City'"—Information provided by James R. Adair in an unpublished manuscript. Used by permission of Dr. Harold Adolph.

"Rickenbacker and the Seagull"—The story has been published in many places, among them Frank C. Laubach, *Prayer, the Mightiest Force in the World* (Old Tappan, N.J.: Revell, 1966).

"Why the Baker Couldn't Sleep"—More information on this story is in George Müller, *The Life of Trust* (London: Gould

and Lincoln, 1873), and Roger Steer, *George Müller: Delighted in God* (Wheaton: Harold Shaw, 1975).

Chapter 7: Out of the Ordinary

"I Want Three Ripe Tomatoes, John"—Taken from the files of the Africa Inland Mission.

"Does God Care about Angel Food Loaf Cakes?"—The complete story is in Jamie Miller, Laura Lewis, and Jennifer Basye Sander, *The Magic of Christmas Miracles* (New York: William Morrow, 1998).

"Send Us a Hot Water Bottle This Afternoon, Lord"—Condensed from Don and Vera Hillis, *God, You, and That Man with Three Goats* (Roanoke, Va., self-published). Used by permission of the authors, 3307 Thurman Ave, Roanoke, VA 24012.

"Following a Little Bird"—Derived from Rosalind Goforth, *How I Know God Answers Prayer* (Nappanee, Ind.: Evangel, 2001).

"Blue Coats and a Flashing Blue Light"—Adapted from the *Adventist Review*, September 1998 (Review and Herald Publishing, Hagerstown, Md.). Used by permission.

"Exactly Five Pounds of Potatoes"—More information on this story can be found in Betty Malz, *Angels Watching over Me* (Grand Rapids: Revell, 1986), and in Joan Wester Anderson, *Where Angels Walk* (New York: Barton and Brett, 1992).

"Honey, Go Buy Those Bluebonnets"—Adapted from Lil Copan and Elisa Fryling, *Finding God between a Rock and a Hard Place* (Wheaton: Harold Shaw, 1999). Used by permission of Jeanie Miley.

Chapter 8: Everyone Talks about the Weather, But . . .

"The Pilgrims' Weather Report"—Much of the background material from Peter

Marshall and David Manuel, *The Light and the Glory* (Grand Rapids: Revell, 1977).

"Astrup's Rain"—Based on story in Fulton Oursler, *Lights along the Shore* (New York: Doubleday, 1954).

"Why the French Invasion Never Happened"—Information derived from David Balsiger, Joettte Whims, and Melody Hunskor, *The Incredible Power of Prayer* (Wheaton: Tyndale, 1998).

"The Christians Carried Umbrellas"—Background information from Harold Lindsell, *When You Pray* (Wheaton: Tyndale, 1969).

"How God Answered Prayer on D-Day"—Much of the information derived from Balsiger, Whims, and Hunskor, *The Incredible Power of Prayer.*

"George Müller in a Fog"—Background material from Roger Steer, *George Müller: Delighted in God* (Wheaton: Harold Shaw, 1975), and A. Naismith, *1200 Notes and Anecdotes* (Chicago: Moody, 1962).

"Watchman Nee and the Island of Mei-Hwa"—Based on material in Robert J. Morgan, *More Real Stories for the Soul* (Nashville: Thomas Nelson, 2000).

Chapter 9: Lost Sheep and the Searching Shepherd

"The Face in the Photo Section"—Derived from various sources. For the full story, see Steve Davis, "Out of the Sky," in *The Miracle of Prayer: True Stories from Guideposts Magazine* (New York: Crescent, 1991).

"The NAACP and the Klan"—More information can be found in Jim Covell, Karen Covell, and Victorya Michaels Rogers, *The Day I Met God* (Portland: Multnomah, 2001).

"What Happens When Mothers Pray"—Another retelling of the story is in Archer Wallace, *Mothers of Famous Men* (New York: Richard R. Smith, 1931).

"The Prayers of 'Little Bilney'"—Background for the story is in F. W. Boreham, *A Bunch of Everlastings* (New York: Abingdon, 1920).

"The Depression of Mordecai Ham"—Basic information from Edward E. Ham, *50 Years on the Battle Front with Christ* (Lexington, Ky.: Old Kentucky Home Revivalist, 1950).

"The Detective Had No Clothes"—Adapted from James Hefley, *Living Miracles* (Grand Rapids: Zondervan, 1964). Used by permission of the author.

"He Kept on Praying for Fifty-Two Years"—Story is derived from Roger Steer, *George Müller: Delighted in God* (Wheaton: Harold Shaw, 1975).

"The Miracle That Didn't Happen"—Adapted from James Hefley, *Living Miracles.* Used by permission of the author.

"He Had Heard It All Before"—Information gleaned from Evelyn Bence, *Spiritual Moments with the Great Hymns* (Grand Rapids: Zondervan, 1997), and from conversations with Jack Luckey.

Chapter 10: People You May Know

"Brother Andrew's Prayer: Lord, Make Seeing Eyes Blind"—Based on Brother Andrew, *God's Smuggler* (New York: The New American Library, 1967).

"Bill Bright's Prayer: Confirm the Vision, Lord"—For more background, see Michael Richardson, *Amazing Faith* (Colorado Springs: Waterbrook, 2000).

"Mother Teresa's Prayer: Only You"—From a number of sources, including Diane Forrest, *The Adventurers* (Nashville: Upper Room, 1983).

"Billy Graham's Prayer: Oh God, Use Me a Little Bit"—Taken from several biographies, including Billy Graham, *Just As I Am* (San Francisco: HarperSanFrancisco, 1997).

"Francis Schaeffer's Prayer: Father, Show Us What to Do"—Derived from various sources including Edith Schaeffer, *The Tapestry* (Waco: Word, 1981).

"Catherine Marshall's Prayer: I Am Beaten, I Am Whipped, I Am Through"—Compiled from several sources.

"C. S. Lewis's Prayer: He Was the Hunter, I Was the Deer"—Compiled from several sources, including C. S. Lewis, *Surprised by Joy* (New York: Harcourt Brace Jovanovich, 1955).

"Charles Colson's Prayer: Somehow I Want to Give Myself to You"—Condensed and adapted from Charles Colson, *Born Again* (Grand Rapids: Chosen, 1976).

Chapter 11: Who Needs to Be a Millionaire?

"Saved by Two Carloads of Cattle"—The complete story is in Howard Hendricks, *Standing Together* (Sisters, Ore.: Multnomah, 1995).

"Delivery Service for Billy Bray"—More on Billy Bray in William W. Patton, *Prayer and Its Remarkable Answers* (Cleveland: Lauer and Mattell, 1892).

"The Hour of Decision for the *Hour of Decision*"—Adapted from Keith J. Hardman, *Seasons of Refreshing* (Grand Rapids: Baker, 1994).

"The Cast-Iron Stove"—Background for the story is in J. C. Pollock, *Hudson Taylor and Maria* (Grand Rapids: Zondervan, 1962).

"Running Out of Miracles?"—Based on information in Harald Bredesen and James F. Scheer, *Need a Miracle?* (Old Tappan, N.J.: Revell, 1979).

"Building on a Better Foundation"—Derived from Henry Blackaby and Claude King, *Experiencing God* (Nashville: Broadman and Holman, 1994).

"Ask Jesus More Often"—Adapted from Basil Miller, *Answered Prayers on the Mission Field* (Grand Rapids: Zondervan, 1955).

"Bologna and Burritos"—Background information derived from Peter Shockey,

Reflections of Heaven (New York: Doubleday, 1999), and from conversations with John and Elizabeth Sherrill.

"How Did I Ever Get into This?"—The Cymbala story is told in Jim Cymbala with Dean Merrill, *Fresh Wind, Fresh Fire* (Grand Rapids: Zondervan, 1997).

Chapter 12: I Didn't Know Angels Looked Like That

"Undercover Cops under Angels' Care"—Basic story is from Joan Wester Anderson, *Where Angels Walk* (New York: Ballantine, 1992). Additional information from Sergeant Steven Rogers, Dayton, N.Y.

"The Hidden Bible"—Derived from Corrie ten Boom, *A Prisoner and Yet* (London: Christian Literature Crusade, 1954).

"Guarded by the Lord's Host"—From a number of sources, including Rosalind Goforth, *How I Know God Answers Prayer* (Nappanee, Ind.: Evangel, 2001).

"You Never Know When You Might Need It"—Derived from Anderson, *Where Angels Walk.*

"Singing in the Skies"—Background story is from Olive Fleming Liefeld, *Unfolding Destinies* (Grand Rapids: Zondervan, 1990).

"Not Exactly Angelic Angels"—Story is adapted from Dan and Vera Hillis, *God, You, and That Man with Three Goats* (Roanoke, Va., self-published). Used by permission of the authors, 3307 Thurman Ave, Roanoke, VA 24012.

"The Bottomless Canyon"—For the complete story, see Marilynn Carlson Webber and William D. Webber, *A Rustle of Angels* (Grand Rapids: Zondervan, 1994).

Chapter 13: The Touch of the Master's Hand

"Drive-by Praying at the Brothels"—Based on material in Jane Rumph, *Stories from the Front Lines* (Grand Rapids: Chosen, 1996; Fairfax, Va.: Xulon, 2001). Used by permission of the author. All rights reserved.

"The Healing Judge"—Adapted from Harald Bredesen and James F. Scheer, *Need a Miracle?* (Old Tappan, N.J.: Revell, 1979).

"Can You Pray for a Horse?"—Background information from several sources, including Stanley Ayling, *John Wesley* (Cleveland: Collins, 1979).

"The Pastor Who Lost His Voice"—Information from several sources but primarily Duane Miller, *Out of the Silence* (Nashville: Thomas Nelson, 1996).

"The Case of the Reluctant Healer"—Based on material in Rumph, *Stories from the Front Lines*. Used by permission of the author. All rights reserved.

"'You Can't,' They Said, but She Did"—Based on numerous sources, including Rodney Clapp, "One Who Took Up Her Bed and Walked," *Christianity Today*, 16 December 1983, 16; Lawrence Brewer, "Healing Touch of Jesus," *Christian Citizen Newsmagazine*, October 1981, 34; correspondence with Barbara Cummiskey; and the files of James R. Adair.

"The Resurrection of Khev Choen"—Based on material in Rumph, *Stories from the Front Lines*. Used by permission of the author. All rights reserved.

"We Can't Spare You Yet"—Derived from a number of sources, including Elon Foster, *6000 Sermon Illustrations* (Grand Rapids: Baker, 1993).

"Go to IHOP"—Story is from Irving King's tapes. Adapted by permission.

Chapter 14: When Even the Road Map Seems Mixed Up

"Tall Order for a Little Woman"—Adapted from various sources, including Helen Kooiman Hosier, *100 Christian Women Who Changed the Twentieth Century* (Grand Rapids: Revell, 2000).

"Betty Greene and Her Flying Machine"—Information from Janet and Geoff Benge, *Betty Greene: Wings to Serve* (Seattle: YWAM Publishing, 1999).

"With a Baseball Bat in His Car"—Condensed and adapted from Peter Shockey, *Reflections of Heaven* (New York: Doubleday, 1999).

"Is Now the Time to Turn Back?"—Information from V. Raymond Edman, *In Step with God* (Chicago: Moody, 1965).

"Mr. Creator, Who Made the Peanut?"—Adapted from S. Graham and D. G. Lipscomb, *Dr. George Washington Carver, Scientist* (Agincourt, Toronto: Book Society of Canada, 1944).

"Getting Away from It All"—Based on material from *Wondrous Power, Wondrous Love*, compiled by the editors of *Decision* magazine (Minneapolis: World Wide Publications, 1983); and correspondence with the author. Used by permission of Christine Wood.

"The Rise of a Rose"—Based on material in A. Kenneth Curtis, ed., *Glimpses* (Worchester, Pa: Christian History Institute, Nov. 2001).

"The Hills Are Alive"—Adapted from Russell Chandler, *The Overcomers* (Old Tappan, N.J.: Revell, 1978).